HORACE MANN AND OTHERS

CHAPTERS FROM THE HISTORY OF ANTIOCH COLLEGE

by Robert Lincoln Straker

with a Preface and an Introduction
to the Antiochiana Collection
in the Olive Kettering Library

by

LOUIS FILLER

THE ANTIOCH PRESS «» 1963

LINE ILLUSTRATIONS BY J. R. HUBBARD
BASED UPON PHOTOGRAPHS
IN THE ANTIOCHIANA COLLECTION.

Contents

Robert Lincoln Straker: An Appreciation

By LOUIS FILLER

There are unlikely to be two Bob Strakers identified with Antioch College, in this generation. This is not merely because it has in recent decades been too much concerned for the present to be concerned for the past. Present-mindedness has characterized the rest of the country, too; and, as someone once remarked, Antioch and Yellow Springs are essentially like other American places and institutions . . . but in a different way. Like America at large, the College has become more receptive to the uses of history, of precedent, in short, of human experience. There is a comfortable number of "history majors" among the student body, and the majority of students, whatever their "majors," tend to be respectful toward the subject-matter of history. Nevertheless, a Bob Straker is not projected, or even molded. He is a product of circumstances and of inner needs. Antioch College has produced and is producing a substantial number of famous and distinguished alumni. None of them has quite accomplished what he, by patient and particular efforts, accomplished for his College, and for scholarship in general.

There is a photograph of Straker as an undergraduate which I find personally pleasing, and in some ways touching, as are all artifacts of the past. It shows him with his fine head of hair, darker than in the photograph here reproduced, and parted in the middle. He looks "smart," to these sentimental eyes, and quite Twenties, though I would not for a moment identify him with ukuleles and a regard for the popular movie stars of the time. Life at Antioch in the 1920's was real and earnest, probably more so than else-

3

where. I will go further and suggest that Straker probably took more seriously and personally the spirit which pervaded the campus, and the principles which its president, Arthur E. Morgan, pressed and exemplified, than did many of his contemporaries. Straker, at this stage of his career, was neither intensively contemporary nor fervently in opposition to his times. Perhaps because of his grassroots origins and sense of the American past, he took the then present as he found it, and measured it judiciously against events which had earlier affected American life.

Straker came of varied stock and from one of the country's crossroads. There were English and Germans in his background. Later, it pleased him to copy passages from books which referred to his pioneer ancestors, and deeds and other courthouse records involving them in Kansas, Virginia, Tennessee, Pennsylvania, and especially North Carolina and his own native Ohio. He was born in 1899 in Versailles, in southwest Ohio—"Versayls" carrying a midwestern pronunciation. His father was a farmer and he himself was born in a loghouse, not much more than fifty miles from Yellow Springs. Straker was raised on a farm and was enough of a boy to have wished that there had been more time for football and other such activities. The greatest adventure of his youth was coming to Antioch, where he manifested an interest in English, as well as in Geology; he was a departmental assistant in the latter area. He was also a formidable member of the student body and a friend of some of the faculty. He edited the *Antiochian* and the *Towers* and founded the *Blaze*, which has a somewhat Paul Revere-ish significance in local community government history.

Straker for a year taught English and "The Nature of the World and of Man" at Wentworth Institute in Boston. I have his lecture notes before me: a pellucid outline from its title-page, which could be readily set up in type, to its indexes and bibliographies. Straker had a strikingly well-ordered and deliberate cast to his mind, and his notebook foreshadows his remarkable labors of later vintage.

4

For two years he was the managing editor of medical magazines. In 1928, he first entered into the work which for the most part engaged him for over thirty years. He joined the Textbook Department of Longmans, Green and Company, in New York, and for four years was involved, as he once had occasion to note, with "personnel, sales, work with authors, etc." He interrupted these labors in 1931 to become a graduate student in Geology at Harvard University, where he assisted Professor Kirtley F. Mather. Straker concluded that the field was not for him. In 1933-1934, he was home at Antioch College, engaged in research in College history, involved in the operations of the Antioch Press, and editor of the *Antioch Alumni Bulletin*.

In terms of his unique achievement, this was the most significant year of his life. In this time, he perceived what work there was to be done in the history of Antioch College: its leading figures, its principles, and, above all, its distinguished founder, Horace Mann. There is some reason to believe that part of the inspiration he experienced derived from the example of vision and action which President Arthur E. Morgan was then providing. In any event, Straker now wrote some of his most informal essays, reflecting his curiosity, his awareness of personalities and novelties of bygone eras, his appreciation of institutions and their directors. Many of his articles appeared in the *Antioch Alumni Bulletin*, several of the best of these—written with ease, grasp, and imagination—are here reproduced. Their major characteristic is that they are written with affectionate concern for local affairs, but with a feeling for the human and the true which makes them immediately meaningful to anyone whose sympathies extend beyond his close and personal concerns.

In 1934, Straker became field representative and assistant manager in the College Text Department of Longmans, Green and Company. As such, he travelled extensively in the middle west. He built up a considerable acquaintanceship with college professors, becoming the personal friend of a number of them, and he developed his habit of visiting libraries to discover what materials they might have which might bear on his interest in Antioch College and its significant personalities. Needless to say, he maintained regular contact with his College and built up a feeling of identification with its personnel and operations which was wholly unique, at a time which saw Antioch (like other institutions) struggling for life in the depths of the greatest depression in American history. Straker, without strain, without projecting special energies or untoward demands upon official attention, became a kind of one-man link between Antioch's past and its present, and, indeed, its relationship with past and present America.

In 1994, Straker had occasion to take account of where he stood as scholar and researcher. He had "done a considerable amount of self-directed reading . . . in American History of the 19th Century," and also had "read hundreds of books and articles, and a vast amount of original material, and [had] made careful notes." This quiet understatement failed to indicate how many hundred books and articles he had mastered, and what careful notes he had taken. In 1940, Straker married and later settled in Yonkers, New York, where his interests and family affairs were arranged in happy balance.

By then, Straker had developed a rich schedule of historical activities. He corresponded with bookdealers, with possessors of original materials bearing on his interests, with librarians, with other researchers, and with the descendents of Antioch personalities, as well as with contemporary Antioch officials interested in utilizing or preserving College records in various ways. With great deliberation, Straker set out to organize his truly voluminous notes. He began with Horace Mann, concerning himself for that educator's ancestors, social circumstances, business and political affairs, personal relations, and whatever else came up in the course of continuing research, reading, correspondence, and individual meetings. All such matters were turned into materials which were carefully typed, recorded in sequence, and revised as newer information required. Straker was no recluse. He gave full attention to his duties as a textbook editor, enjoyed his academic contacts, and did his duty conscientiously—perhaps too conscientiously—as a reader of proofs. He concerned himself, too, for his men in the field, after 1939, when he became editor and sales manager of the College Text Department of his company.

Also, Straker was far from being an inept intellectual. He could fix anything, his wife thought. At home, he made three rooms into a splendid one, manufactured a distinctive table, and created a front door where there had been a lavatory. At their summer home in South Amherst, Massachusetts, his son recalls: "He cleared the land where the cottage now stands and may have played a part in its construction. The adjoining field (about ten acres) was made more farmable by a drainage ditch he dug: a submerged tile drainage." There is much more that could be added to indicate that Straker was a man who worked with his hands as well as his mind, and for love and associates as well as intellectual interests.

The Mann project matured, in Straker's conception, into projects involving Mann and his family, and his co-workers, and Antioch College as a whole. The notes on all of these flourished in every chronological and topical direction. They never became in the least disorganized. Straker procured new binders for holding together the augmented materials. He evolved systems for cross-references and indexes. By 1944, he was prepared to project a "comprehensive biography of Horace Mann . . . based on considerable fresh material; planned to present a study of his private and public character, his personality and his accomplishments as a lawyer, legislator, educator, reformer, and humanitarian; with proper attention to his contemporaries and to the social, economic, and political history of the period."

Was there ever a possibility that Straker might actually have consummated such a work? Straker published a number of excellent essays and documents in the field, and prepared several which he did not trouble to put into print. He later drew up several chapters for the projected Mann biography dealing with aspects of his subject's career, and these can be ultimately organized for publication. They will be welcomed by scholars. Nevertheless, I doubt seriously that Straker could have brought himself to finish his biography of Mann, or written one of Elizabeth P. Peabody, or prepared a history of Antioch College, and simply because his work as a researcher and evaluator of evidence and circumstances was a creative act. There was always so much more that could be uncovered! Straker could not resist an unexplored byway, whether it involved genealogy—always fascinating to him—social customs, the warp and woof of administration, anecdotes, or ideas. I append a paragraph from a letter by Straker—he was never too busy to deal with correspondents or to help other students of his subject—which offers some sense of his extraordinary concern for details; the following is from a ten-page letter, single-spaced:

> Mann had a fundamental incapacity to meet the complicated requirements of his work as President.—This is the nub of your article—that he was too strict in discipline and lacked an understanding of adolescent and mature psychology. There is no doubt that his discipline was strict—Theodore Parker said that he was too austere to succeed as a college president—but he was strict partly because he did understand the social and psychological aspects of student life. Parker was austere himself, though less so than Mann. Dr. S. G. Howe also believed Mann was too austere, and Howe was less so than Mann. But I wonder how Parker or Howe would have handled the *Probe* incident. Or President Fairchild of Oberlin? Or even President Tappan himself, had the University of Michigan been a coeducational college?
>
> Mann was offered the presidency of several other colleges, including Butler University, Union Christian, the State University of Iowa, the University of Wisconsin, and several others, including a Missouri college, probably Palmyra (1839). But these offers came in large part because of his towering reputation, but also in part because of the job he had done at Antioch and Antioch's then current difficulties. A great many of his contemporaries obviously did not regard him as temperamentally unfitted for a college presidency.

Dr. A. E. Morgan is very much like Mann, and he had had some very good offers of presidencies too.

With such concern for nuances of interpretation, there was scarcely an occasion for Straker to complete his labors. The truth was that the field he had chosen was desperately underdeveloped. With all the Schools of Education, and despite the proliferation of theses in the area, there had been too little joining of issues, in terms of what American experience with education revealed. Straker could not properly complete his work because the entire substratum of his theme had to be laid. In some twenty-five years of patient, absorbed, and wholly satisfactory researches, Straker almost single-handedly laid the base for study of American education, at least in terms of his great protagonist.[1]

Straker continued his researches, maintained his contacts with Antioch College, where he found particular appreciation from Dean W. Boyd Alexander. His generosity with ideas and invaluable information never failed, except in cases when he felt that his subjects were being exploited without conscience. In a typical communication, sent in 1956, he advised a nun interested in preparing a thesis on Mann. He informed her that there had been some twenty-five master's theses done, and about ten doctoral dissertations, and that those he had seen were not worth a second glance. "The field for serious study is fairly wide open." He went on to offer suggestions, based conscientiously on his correspondent's limited travel and costs resources. He went on to comment on various library holdings:

> May I say that I am myself much concerned over the constant shredding which the Mann papers in the Massachusetts Historical Society Library must be undergoing constantly? I have done my share, for I have been through them twice myself, and ———————— has probably built a nest in them.

His gracious solution was to place a copy of his Mann Notes

---

[1] See my description of Antiochiana, pp. 97 ff., for an analysis of his achievement.

and Peabody Notes, "both fully indexed, . . . in the Mass. Hist. Soc. Library if it can be done with the understanding that they will be freely open to persons like yourself. . . ."

Straker's charm was often noted, but Straker was more than charming. He was fair and dependable: a person on whom his colleagues could build. One, having no axe to grind of any sort, and, indeed, concerned only for aiding in Straker's vindication in a painful business crisis which had arisen—in itself a remarkable act, in the New York setting—had occasion to write him as follows:

> I think there is no way I can compliment you slyly so I shall have to do it directly. In my life I've never met a person finer than you. I'll probably never have a better boss for the rest of my life. ————————————————— just said that I'm doing the right thing, that I shouldn't go on just for mercenary reasons (which are particularly important to us right now), and that this is a case where ". . . the boss made the job.". . . Your simple axiom, that better profits come with better books, may not be entirely true, that is, exclusively, but it was the only one I could work with. . . . These general feelings, and the notion that my resignation might by one jot vindicate you . . . , leaves just the one course open to me now.

Straker left his old firm and spent a pleasant and profitable, if brief, period at Scribner's Sons, also in its textbook department. I met one of his associates, following his death in 1959, at a meeting of the American Historical Association. I had no reason to mention Straker and noted only that I was from Antioch College. I spent a most remarkable hour listening to praise of Straker, from one who had been shy of voicing his admiration of the man while he was still alive. It was an unrehearsed tribute of the kind that any human being might cherish.

With the poet Stephen Spender, Straker might have said, "I think continuously of those who are truly great." He himself was not of the glamorously immortal, but neither was he one of the spiders who spin and spin and who must be interpreted in terms of instincts and compulsions. Straker had a vision. It was a vision of great people and noble aspirations. In that vision, too, was an institution which glowed with purpose and which was to be perennially renewed with fresh generations of youth. Straker's achievement is secure. It lies on sound ground. It is broad-based and amply supported. The building which rests upon it will not be his, but Straker never thought that achievement was anything less than a co-operative effort. It sufficed for him that he had contributed to the whole.

HORACE MANN AND OTHERS

1

The Master Builder from Massachusetts

MERRIFIELD AND THE FOUNDING OF ANTIOCH COLLEGE

Writing in the February 8, 1851, issue of the *Christian Palladium*, Elijah Shaw, a prominent Christian minister of central New York, said of the infant Antioch College: "Before the proposed edifice shall moulder to dust on its foundations, a hundred millions may be swarming on our soil, to be succeeded by another hundred millions every thirty years."

The Christian Connexion, a religious body which arose in various eastern states at the dawn of the nineteenth century, was said to differ from the Unitarians only in that it had a better name. A real difference existed, however, in the Christian's advocacy of vigorous proselytism through revivals and prayer-meetings of an emotional nature. The Christians, despite their professed liberalism, were at times bigoted and narrow and were for many decades distrustful of education, even for the ministry. But the prospects before a vast, expanding country, with a rapidly increasing population, gradually convinced the Christians that their duty lay in promoting education among themselves.

Bonds of fellowship between the Christians and the Unitarians appeared at an early period and soon grew strong. As early as 1837, Dr. Channing urged upon the Christians "the importance of fortifying themselves with educational establishments." In 1840 Isaac N. Walter, a minister of western Ohio, advocated the founding of a Christian college in the Ohio valley. The more liberal of the Christians joined with the Unitarians in organizing the Meadville Theological School in 1844. In the same year Simon Clough, Christian minister in New York City, urged his denomination to establish both a university and a Biblical school. Interest in a Christian institution of learning increased during the next few years, with enthusiastic support from the sectarian press.

During 1849 and 1850 Alpheus Marshall Merrifield, a building contractor of Worcester, Massachusetts, visited widely among the Christians in New York and New England, urging upon them the importance and practicability of founding a first-class college. Others were active in the same cause in other parts of the country.

Merrifield was born in Worcester, May 25, 1809. His father was for many years a deacon of the Second Parish Church, a highly respected citizen. From his father he learned carpentry and building and worked with him for several years. While still a young man he went to Conneaut, Ohio, and there engaged in construction work. He was here "converted" by Elder Oliver Barr of the Christian Connexion, and became a member of that denomination. About 1840 he returned to Worcester, purchased a large tract of timbered land on what is now Laurel Hill, divided it into building lots, and himself built several houses there. From 1843 to 1859 inclusive, his name appears in the Worcester directories as a carpenter. He seems to have had no special training as an architect, though he may have studied privately. By his fellow-Christians Merrifield was deemed to be a man of considerable wealth and unusual business ability. He was referred to proudly as "the master-builder from Massachusetts." His interest in education was warmly welcomed and eagerly supported, and he at once became one of the leaders in the college movement.

Many urged the inclusion of both literary and theological departments, worthy of the best patronage, so that Christian youth might not be lost to the denomination through attendance at other sectarian colleges.

On May 8 and 9, 1850, an informally chosen committee on education, of which Merrifield was a member, met in New York City to formulate a plan for a college, a plan to be laid before a meeting of delegates from Christian congregations in the United States and Canada, to be held at Marion, Orange County, New York, October 2, 1850. In this plan were embodied most of the features of the institution later founded by the Christians—Antioch College.

The delegates assembled at Marion and organized the convention. On the afternoon of October 5, Dr. J. R. Freese, secretary of the convention, presented a resolution: "Resolved, that our responsibility to the community and the advancement of our interests as a denomination demand of us the establishment of a College." Merrifield was among those who arose to address the convention in support of this resolution. The delegates adopted the measure unanimously. The phrase "our interests as a denomination," was later held by the advocates of theological training to show the support of the convention for such a department.

The committee on education laid its plans before the convention. A new committee, which included Merrifield, adopted the plan as presented and suggested the formation of a provisional committee (thirty-four members) to supervise generally the whole project, and a sub-committee (thirteen members) to raise funds, locate and build the college, and serve as trustees until a regularly elected board could be chosen. The committee resolved that equal educational privileges should be extended to both sexes. It is to be noted that no resolution or suggestion was ever presented or adopted making the proposed college non-sectarian. Most of the eighty-two delegates to the Marion convention were doubtless in favor of a denominational college, since at that time nearly all colleges were denominational. Antioch became non-sectarian through the influence of the more liberal leaders (Fay, Wait, Millard, Craig, and others), some of whom later became Unitarian ministers.

Although Merrifield spoke little in the Marion convention, he had much to do with shaping its counsels. He was chosen treasurer of the sub-committee and as such served as first treasurer of the college. He was also one of the heaviest contributors to the new institution, giving $1,000 to the college.

During the year following the Marion convention interest in the proposed college ran high. It was freely predicted that Antioch would change the destiny of the human race. Although solicitors were busy elsewhere, none compared with John Phillips of Lebanon who raised in Ohio without assistance six times as much money as was gathered in all the other states together. He heaped ridicule upon those in New England and New York who were deserting the cause, suggesting that they go over to the Baptists—"they can be spared!" He boasted with characteristic overstatement that southwestern Ohio alone could build a dozen Antiochs, and astounded his listeners with the declaration that "the great Antioch telescope will be placed on such a high tower that we can see Lake Erie, and the people in the streets of New Orleans!"[1]

---

[1] Such a tower would have to be about eighty miles high.

The sub-committee met in Stafford, Genesee County, New York, October 29, 1851. Merrifield was placed on two committees —that on location, to visit proposed sites, and that on drafts and estimates, to secure plans and costs for the college buildings. In recognition of the support of Ohio, it was decided to locate the college in that state.

The committee on location then visited each of the eight Ohio communities which asked for the college—Conneaut, Mt. Vernon, Lebanon, New Carlisle, Eaton, Milton, Union, and Yellow Springs—and reported to the sub-committee at Enon, Ohio, January 21, 1852. The committee on drafts and estimates recommended the construction of three buildings—a main building and "male" and "female" dormitories. As moving spirit of the committee, Merrifield presented plans for the three structures, "magnificent buildings, excelling anything west of the Alleghenies." The sub-committee then "Resolved, that the thanks of this committee be tendered to Messrs. Kyler and Knoll for furnishing plans for the College gratuitously." It is probable that Merrifield designed the buildings and that Kyler and Knoll merely drew the plans according to his suggestions. A photograph of Merrifield, as the architect, was placed in the cornerstone of Antioch Hall (northeast octagonal tower).

The sub-committee met again five days later in Yellow Springs and, inspecting the stump-filled wheat field which was to be the campus, chose the site of Antioch Hall. Many thought the buildings were to be too large and costly, but the leaders planned for an enrollment of 1,000. For the time and place it was indeed a daring project. Antioch Hall was to be the largest building in the state, located at the highest point of land in Ohio![2] And what hopes for improving mankind were placed in the new college!

Many supporters of the college wished to include theological training. Little evidence of opposition is found, but such there

[2] Elevation, 1,000 feet. The highest point in the state, 1,550 feet, is near Bellefontaine.

must have been, for by the time of the sub-committee meeting on January 26 sufficient strength had been gathered to close the curriculum to theological study. It was then decided to take steps at once to raise money and establish a theological school independent of the college. Merrifield, giving $500, was the first contributor. But with the death of Elder Barr, chief advocate of the school, the movement came to an end. The attempt of the sectarians to make Antioch denominational had not yet ended, however.

Eli Fay, of the Committee on Faculty, was able to approach Horace Mann regarding the presidency of Antioch with the assurance that the new college would be both coeducational and non-sectarian. These two features, rare in those days, persuaded Mann to accept the offer.

Merrifield was one of the seven members appointed to the building committee. Almost the only act of this committee was to name Merrifield building agent, with full power to represent the committee—to make contracts, provide materials, and oversee the work. He immediately secured several thousand dollars' worth of materials and engaged laborers, masons, and carpenters. Local malcontents who opposed the whole college project as a snobbish move caused Merrifield some confusion and delay by moving the stakes on the sites of the building. The work, however, was pushed forward with great vigor.

The provisional committee met in Yellow Springs on May 12-14, 1852. All were pleased with the location, with the progress made, and with the ability of the building agent. It is probable that Horace Mann attended this meeting, for he visited Yellow Springs at this time, and it was known in June that he would accept the presidency.

On September 15 the sub-committee met in Yellow Springs to view the campus and buildings and to go over the situation with Merrifield. As building agent, Merrifield was instructed to prepare plans for a dwelling for the president of the college. A faculty was also formally engaged—President Mann and six professors (September 17).

Confidence in the future of the college and the village was unlimited. Judge Mills laid out town lots in great numbers, confidently expecting Yellow Springs to become a city of at least 10,000. There was so much money in prospect that Merrifield as treasurer kept inadequate accounts or no accounts at all. When he was offered the services of a bookkeeper for $400 a year, he declared that such expense would be wholly wasted.[3]

The dedication of the college and the inauguration of the president on October 5, 1853, found grounds ungraded and everything in confusion. Scaffolding stood about Antioch Hall, finished except for the towers. The rooms in North Hall were ready for occupancy, though heat was not yet provided. South Hall and the President's House were not completed until the autumn of 1854.[4]

The dormitories may be dismissed as being without architectural style. The President's House (burned in 1924), square, with cupola and encircling veranda, was typical of the larger dwellings of the day. Antioch Hall seems to be almost *sui generis*, for there are very few large buildings in America at all resembling it.[5] Possibly the architect sought to include a feeling of the Levant, appropriate to the name of Antioch. The style has been called Moorish, Gothic, Colonial, Queen Anne, Flemish Romanesque, Victorian Gothic, Antiochian, and Inverted Billiard Table.

With the completion of the buildings and the imminent discharge of the sub-committee came the election of a permanent Board of Trustees on September 4, 1854. Merrifield was named

---

[3] Later it was found that his negligence had created so much confusion that not even an estimate of the college indebtedness could be made. There is no indication of dishonesty. Lack of competent accounting was inexcusable, but the real trouble was insufficient income. Merrifield, along with many others, lost considerable money through his connection with the college.

[4] Merrifield had at first estimated the total cost of the college buildings at $50,000; after construction was begun he raised the estimate to $60,000. The final cost was placed at $120,000.

[5] Holy Cross Academy, Worcester; Deane Academy, Franklin, Mass.; and Orton Hall, Ohio State University.

a trustee and served for the next three years, although Judge Mills succeeded him as treasurer. During the seven years of his intimate association with the college, from 1850 to 1857, he was among the two or three leaders, if not the foremost of them all. After the buildings were begun, his leadership was still further strengthened, for then he was on the ground at the center of activities. It was to Merrifield that Mann wrote regarding the plans of the trustees for the college, and other trustees consulted him frequently. He was clearly a man of strength and drive, firmly committed to his own convictions. He had striven for the inclusion of theological training, for example, and later when dissension arose he was found in the camp of the denominationalists.

By the close of the second college year in 1855 antagonism had begun to develop between the liberals in education, headed by President Mann, and the conservatives in religion, whose champion was Professor Ira W. Allen. Soon after coming to Yellow Springs Mann had joined the local Christian Church and sincerely sought religious fellowship with the Christians, although he continued to oppose revivals and looked with disfavor upon prayer meetings. He proposed to present to the college students the features of all religions, emphasizing the ethical and moral aspects. The sectarians, however, feared this plan because they said it would "Unitarianize" the college, and they still sought to make Antioch denominational. Opponents of this sinewy, unrelenting stamp always fought to the last ditch. Mann moved forward with the inevitability of a glacier, while Allen, supported by Merrifield and to some extent by Judge Mills and Elder Ladley of the Yellow Springs Christian Church, set about in wily fashion to gain sufficient strength among the trustees to have Mann discharged and Allen appointed to the presidency.

The quarrel became bitter and personal. Ladley asserted that a hundred students had become infidels under Mann's tutelage, though when asked to do so he preferred not to name any of them. Merrifield hovered in the background, quietly marshalling support among the trustees. A test of strength came at the trustees' meeting on September 1, 1856, at the election of a principal of the preparatory department. Mann's candidate was John C. Zachos, then acting principal. Merrifield's choice was Henry D. Burlingame, who had resigned from the faculty a few months before in protest against the discharge of his fiancée, Josephine Chamberlain, for incompetency and incompatibility. The vote of the trustees showed two-thirds in favor of Burlingame. Mann asked for a reconsideration, objecting to Burlingame's lack of ability and experience, and added that it would be unpleasant to have him because of his wife. "Mr. Merrifield rose and moved that the Trustees require President Mann and all the married professors to obtain divorces immediately (laughter)."[6] Two-thirds again voted for Burlingame, but he declined to serve.

When the college became bankrupt in the spring of 1857 all the instructors were released. Almost at once, however, it was decided to continue the college for a time until some solution of the financial problem could be found, and the faculty were re-employed, with the exceptions of Professors Allen and Doherty, the former because he was troublesome and the latter because he was incompetent. Merrifield had supported Allen for the Antioch presidency and now stood by while Allen prepared a bitter, slanderous attack upon Mann and his supporters.[7] The struggle seemed, however, to outwear Merrifield's interest and patience. Writing from Worcester on December 7, 1857, to Wm. F. King, clerk of the Antioch Board of Trustees, he resigned:

Gentlemen Sirs,

Believing that I can no longer hold, with honor, to myself, or benefit to the Christian Connexion, the office of Trustee, of Antioch College, I transmit to you this, my resignation of said office.

---

[6] *A History of the Rise, Difficulties and Suspension of Antioch College*, by Prof. Ira W. Allen. Columbus, Geary, 1858.

[7] *Op. cit.*

A reply[8] to Allen's attack was made under the editorship of Elder Eli Fay, and Allen was completely discredited.

Merrifield's last appearance on the Antioch scene was his visit to Yellow Springs for two weeks in the summer of 1858. He criticized the Mann regime severely and strongly advised Christian parents to send their children elsewhere rather than to Antioch.

After completing the construction work at Antioch, Merrifield returned to Worcester and resumed business there. A photograph of him taken about 1865, is extant. It shows a spare figure, thinning sandy hair, lank pointed jaw, high cheek bones, and penetrating hazel eyes.

Sometime between 1859 and 1865 he left Worcester, returning only for infrequent visits. In 1865 he settled in Mattawan, Michigan, and for a few years engaged in building. He left Mrs. Merrifield behind in Worcester and later divorced her. Their two sons, his only children, remained with the mother, and both died childless many years later.

Soon he retired from business, re-married, and lived quietly in Mattawan with his wife and her mother, working in the garden and sitting by the fire while he grew old. His last years were uneventful. His wife, an excellent seamstress, contributed largely to their support. She was active in the Congregational Church, but he took no part in church work, ridiculed all religion, and was looked upon as an "infidel." When a long illness had at last brought him to the end, he refused to heed the entreaties of his friends that he turn to religion for comfort and hope. On June 3, 1891, at the age of eighty-two, he died as he had lived—an unbeliever.

Merrifield was outstanding among the founders of Antioch College. Indeed it is probable that without him "the Mammoth of the West" would never have been founded at all.

---

[8] *A Rejoinder to the Pseudo-History of Antioch College by Professor Allen.* Edited by Eli Fay. Yellow Springs, 1859.

2

Judge Mills

FRIEND OF TOWN AND GOWN

The Duke of Saxe-Weimar, in his *Reise durch Nord-Amerika in dem Jahren 1825-26*, records his visit of a few hours at Yellow Springs on May 8, 1826, while traveling by stage from Cincinnati to Columbus:

> We stopped on our way at a small village, Yellow Springs, to see the spring from which the place derives its name. The village occupies

a woody elevation on the shore of the Little Miami [*sic*], rushing through a deep, rocky valley. The place is small, and was bought by a society of twelve gentlemen, under the direction of Mr. Lowndes. These gentlemen intended to found a sect upon Owen's system; there had been one established here previously, but dissolved on account of the majority of them being worthless creatures, who had brought neither capital, nor inclination to work. Mr. Lowndes, whose acquaintance I made, said that he expected new and better members. The locality is healthful and favorable for such an establishment. The spring originates in a limestone rock, the water has a little taste of iron, and deposits a great quantity of ochre, from which it takes its name. The spring is said to give one hundred and ten gallons of water per minute, which is received in a basin, surrounded by cedar trees. The yellow stream which comes from the basin runs a short distance over a bed of limestone and is afterward precipitated into the valley. These limestone rocks form very singular figures on the edge of the valley; the detached pieces resemble the Devil's Wall of the Hartz. They have no baths fitted up, as yet there is only a shower-bath. The former will most probably be established, when it becomes a place of public resort. Mr. Lowndes told me that it was his intention to take more water in, and to have some walks established in the vicinity, to which the surrounding country is very favorable. [His Highness found the roads extremely muddy, even in May, and was forced to walk most of the way from Clifton to Springfield. —R.L.S.]

The Yellow Spring had been a favorite spot of the Miamis and Shawnees long before the coming of the white man. The water was valued highly for its supposed curative properties. Converging on the spring were several well-worn trails, among them the main path between the Indian villages at Old Town and Piqua. This trail, traversed thousands of times by Tecumseh and his braves, crossed the present college campus, entered the valley by a path still in use, and led northward along the west side of the stream. Even after their transportation to Kansas, the Shawnees returned on horseback to visit the spring, a few coming as late as 1840.

In 1805 Lewis Davis built a log hut on the bluff north of the spring, the first habitation in the vicinity. This house served as store and post-office and later became a part of the large tavern built there. The Owenite community established in a large commons hall near the cascade in the glen in 1825 survived for only a few months. A severe winter brought all of the two hundred members to the verge of starvation, with consequent behavior far from communistic, and the experiment was abandoned. The enterprise of the "twelve gentlemen under the direction of Mr. Lowndes" was never begun. In 1827, the year following the Duke's visit, the Yellow Spring was sold to Elisha Mills of Cincinnati— the spring land selling for $9 an acre, and the adjoining land for $3.50.

Elisha Mills was a native of Connecticut and a descendant of Sir Peter Vander Menlen of Amsterdam, who had been knighted for public services and for his learning. As a young man Elisha had set up as a lawyer in Huntington, Connecticut. His sister Ruth married Owen Brown; in 1805 the Brown family left for Ohio and later moved into Kansas; one of the sons is known to history as John Brown of Ossawatomie and Harper's Ferry. Elisha's son William was born January 5, 1814. The urge to go west seized the Mills family also and in 1822 they went to Illinois. The mother, however, was too frail to endure the hardships of frontier life and soon sickened and died. The family returned to Connecticut by way of the Gulf of Mexico; Elisha remarried and in 1826 brought his family to Cincinnati. The following year found them established at the Yellow Spring.

The children ran and jumped with the Indians when they returned to visit the Spring and pitched their tepees on the western bank of the glen. There were few buildings at the Spring, but Mr. Mills set out to make this, the only summer resort in Ohio, widely known; he spent some $7,000 in building the hotel and laying out the grounds.[1] On March 30, 1829, the Cincinnati papers carried the announcement of the opening of the Watering Place,

---

[1] In Judge Mill's account, this appears as $700,000, but surely this is a case of a missing decimal point. Judge Mills himself sold the Spring and adjoining land in 1841 for $15,000.

Yellow Springs, Ohio, under the direction of Elisha Mills. The Mansion House boasted a piazza two hundred feet long, and there were six cottages, a billiard house, two bowling alleys, and a stable of riding horses. The water was declared to be a specific for dyspepsia. Ague, the curse of the poorly drained frontier, was unknown. There were three stages daily from Cincinnati to Yellow Springs, one through Hamilton and Dayton, and the others through Reading and Lebanon. Mail from Washington and Baltimore was received in five days, from Philadelphia in six, and from New York in seven.

The Watering Place did indeed become widely known; it attracted visitors from Cincinnati, Memphis, New Orleans, and even from New York and New England. In June, 1829, Edward Everett spoke at the spring on the true greatness of Washington—a theme he was to present again and again during the coming twenty years in an attempt to prevent the dissolution of the Union. He spoke of "this lovely spot, where everything seems combined that can delight the eye, afford recreation, and promote health." Other speakers at various times included Henry Clay, Daniel Webster, Gen. Winfield Scott, Wm. Henry Harrison, Salmon P. Chase, and Martin Van Buren.

William Mills prepared for college under Judge Torbet of Springfield; he walked or rode horseback to Springfield once a week for private lessons. At fourteen he was able to do creditable translation from Greek. He entered Kenyon College and became a good classical scholar. Later he transferred to Miami University. His college course was interrupted by the death of his brother in an explosion in the chemical laboratory at Miami; his father withdrew him, probably through fear of a similar accident to him, although he had nearly finished his course. For a time he kept a store on Mad River, near Enon, for his father. When he reached marriageable age, his father gave him six hundred acres of land at Yellow Springs, including the spring land. In 1840 he married Miss Margaretta Poague of Spring Valley; to them was born one daughter, Ellen Mills Hollingshead. His second wife was Mrs. Ann Eliza Marshall Starry; their children were Elisha; William; Ann Eliza (Mrs. W. H. Sloan, Chicago); Julia (Mrs. Edward Chapman, Cleveland); Charles; and Birdie.

In 1840 there were few buildings in Yellow Springs. At about this time William Mills built the first brick house in the village. In 1842 he began the construction of the present Mills House, and occupied it in January, 1843. His father censured him severely for building a fine house in a swamp where the water was frequently three feet deep, but later gave his approval when the ground was drained and landscaped and the Mills House became the show place of the town.[2]

Under a charter dated March 11, 1836, the Little Miami Railroad was organized to build and maintain a railway from Cincinnati, by way of Xenia, to Springfield, where it met the recently constructed National Trail. This was the first railroad built north of the Ohio River. When only twelve miles of track had been laid, funds were exhausted and the work suspended. With the consent of all concerned, young William Mills went to Boston and succeeded in raising $500.00[3]—the first bit of Eastern capital invested in a railroad west of the Alleghenies. In recognition of this great service, the road was laid through Yellow Springs instead of through Clifton, then the largest and most prosperous community in the township. The completed road of eighty-four miles between Cincinnati and Springfield was opened in August, 1846.

William Mills was keenly interested in the industrial development of the village. He built, where the Hughes house now stands

---

[2] Antioch acquired the property in 1921, and for many years it housed the Antioch School. In 1951, after the construction of the new Antioch School building on campus, the large lot containing Mills House was presented to the Yellow Springs School Board, and the Mills Lawn (elementary) School was built on the front part of the lot. Mills House is presently being used by the elementary school for additional classroom space and administrative offices.—L.F.

[3] Half a million—$7,000 a mile—seems a large amount, but considering the road-bed grading necessary, and the probable graft, this was not too much. The first track was strap iron on beams; T-rails were laid in 1848.

on the northeast corner of the athletic field, a three-story machine shop—the largest and best-equipped machine shop in the state at that time. He was eager to have sober and industrious townsmen and to that end championed the temperance cause and, himself an Episcopalian, gave the plots on which were built the Methodist, Christian, Baptist, and Episcopal churches. He opposed slavery and was an enthusiastic supporter of general education. He came to be known as Judge Mills through being retained by county judges to settle ordinary non-legal, local cases.

We find him, then, at the dawn of the year 1852, a man of thirty-eight, happily married and with a growing family, wealthy for his time and place, unusually generous and altruistic, and genuinely interested in the welfare of his fellowmen. Ahead of him lay two nation-wide financial panics, in one of which (1857) he lost his fortune, and in the other (1873) he was again reduced to poverty. Before him also were the misunderstandings and disappointments which marked his labors for Antioch and for other causes near his heart. But at the end of his life, poor and diseased and stripped of everything except the love and respect of family and friends, he was yet able to say that he regretted nothing he had done.

Becoming enthusiastic over the possibility of having Antioch located in Yellow Springs, and with consequent economic and cultural development of the community, the people of the village empowered Judge Mills to represent them before the sub-committee meeting at Enon in January, 1852, and to offer $30,000 and twenty acres for a campus. The location was to be decided on four points: (1) "accessibility by travel," (2) healthfulness, (3) cheapness of living, and (4) the amount given by the community. Judge Mills presented strong arguments in favor of Yellow Springs: the railroad and the stage lines made the village easily accessible by travel; he declared the locality so healthful that those wishing to die had to leave town to do so, and he could truthfully say that living was absurdly cheap. Lebanon offered $40,000 and a twenty-three acre campus, but was ruled out on the other points.

Judge Mills returned to Yellow Springs with the prize, filled with enthusiasm for the whole project. He himself gave the twenty acres for the campus and paid more than $20,000 of the amount pledged. He anticipated a great real estate boom, expecting Yellow Springs to become a city of at least 10,000. He employed a surveyor, Samuel T. Owen, to lay out streets in his three-hundred acre farm, and these streets he graded and graveled, undeterred by Judge Harlan's cynical observation that the gravel would make plowing difficult after the boom had failed. He was willing to take notes instead of cash for his building lots; he received little money, for most of the purchasers took advantage of his trust. Everyone thought the college had unlimited resources, and the bubble grew—chiefly at the expense of Judge Mills.

During the summer of 1853 he was also busily occupied with the construction of a schoolhouse for his children and children of the faculty. This house, modeled after a Swiss chateau, was known as "Little Antioch" because of its fancied resemblance to Antioch Hall. His plans for the school occasioned considerable correspondence with Mr. Mann.

On Dec. 21, 1852, Judge Mills met Mr. Mann in Cincinnati and brought him to Yellow Springs, entertained him, and introduced him to college affairs. In a letter to his wife Mr. Mann said:

> Judge Mills is the right sort of a man; he has got his head cleared of all the old cobwebs. He is a *character*, unpretending in manner, without any great show of force, yet with the active or bilious temperament, has been through the experience of Methodist conversion and has found what they are worth. He is full of sound sense and full of the philosophy of phrenology, talks on religious matters with wisdom. He is capable of wielding an immense amount of influence, does wield it, and by his *sense* and his *money* will be able to stand up against the bigots. It is delightful to think there is such a man there.

A few days later Mrs. Mann wrote: "Thank heaven for Judge Mills. What a godsend he is to you, who are about to leave your 'brain relations' behind you. Let us take it as a good omen."

Judge Mills was among the signers of the articles of incorporation of the college on May 14, 1852. He was elected a member of the first Board of Trustees on September 4, 1854, and served until 1859. He succeeded Mr. Merrifield as treasurer in 1854. In 1856 he became president of the executive committee of the trustees. He was a generous friend of the students; he threw his home open to all, and many were the gay occasions in the mansion in The Park.

Soon it became evident that the college actually had no money at all; fewer families were coming to the village than had been anticipated, and there was but slight demand for Antioch "scholarships." The tide of hope began to reverse itself as the college sank into debt. Judge Mills became increasingly embarrassed financially and on every side was abused by those who were aggrieved over the loss of what they had never possessed. At last, during the panic of 1857, the clamor of creditors drove him to take voluntary bankruptcy, and all his property was held to satisfy his debts. When the sheriff's men came to remove the chattels from the mansion, largely at the demand of Mills' brother-in-law, Col. Joseph Wilson, nothing was spared, not even the china and silver.

Judge Mills still held notes for sums he had loaned the building committee of the college. These were a part of the so-called Reyburn claim. In May, 1858, Eastern friends proposed to loan the college a sum of money, meant as a gift, if Ohio friends would clear the Reyburn claim. Judge Mills found it impossible to trust the good faith of this Eastern offer and thereby ran afoul of President Mann. Then ensued one of the saddest phases of Mills' relationship with the College. He maintained his position despite the strongest logic Mr. Mann was able to marshall against him. Matters soon reached the stage when communication between the two men was by messenger or letter. In May, 1859, Mr. Mann learned through Rev. Fay that Judge Mills planned to go to Cincinnati to have the sale of the college vacated so that he might press his claim. In a letter to him, dated May 27, Mr. Mann wrote: "If you suppose that in this or any other matter, I stand in antagonism to your interest, I assure you you are greatly mistaken. I think you have wronged me, in a late act, but as yet I feel no retaliatory spirit and hope not to." The sale was not vacated (probably Judge Mills never asked for it), and with the bankruptcy of the college his claim lapsed.

Entering the Union Army, Judge Mills became quartermaster of the 74th Ohio Infantry. Assigned one day to the command of a foraging party, he returned to camp empty-handed because he could not bring himself to take food from women and children. Subsequently he was appointed post quartermaster at Nashville and was in charge of the distribution of supplies to the troops in the western region. In this position of trust he was exposed to many temptations of graft, but he remained scrupulously honest and left the army as poor as when he entered. In July, 1864, Mrs. Mills died in Nashville of fever contracted while nursing soldiers.

After being mustered out of the army, he remained in Nashville and for two years served as city recorder; he became director of the state penitentiary and was elected a trustee of Central College. In March 1868, he married Mrs Raiford of Edgefield, Tennessee; they had one daughter, Mary Elena Mills Smith. In 1870 he went to Achinson, Kansas, and set up a real estate business—which was ruined in the panic of 1873. He then went to Chicago and, becoming a partner of George W. Hill, again entered real estate, but once more his business failed. In 1876 he returned to Yellow Springs, afflicted with cystitis. This year he was defeated for the nomination for probate judge of the county. He died at his humble residence in the village on November 3, 1879.

On July 4, 1876, Judge Mills delivered at Xenia the Centennial Historical Address for Greene County. In his account of the history of the county he spoke of the college he had done so much to found and maintain:

> . . . From the Far East to the remote West, young men and women of earnest intention and loftiest aims became its students; and today its graduates are filling posts of honor and usefulness in the various fields of human industry, where literary ability and moral worth are sought as agencies to build up and adorn society, as well as active participants in the great political arena of both our state and national councils. The broad and liberal features of the institution, the world-wide renown of its first president, and the noble work it has already

accomplished have made it well and favorably known, not only in our own land but on the continent of Europe, in all the famous seats of learning and schools of art, from the Louvre to the Vatican, from Leipsig to Berlin. In after years, if not now, it will be claimed as a trophy of richest inheritance that within the limits of Greene County was located Antioch College, and such and such statesmen and scholars went forth from her halls, and that the great commoner of universal education and one of the greatest advocates of human rights and all practical reforms, the late Hon. Horace Mann, lived and died here in the midst of his world-wide usefulness.

3

The Years of Exile

HORACE MANN AT ANTIOCH (1853-1859)

Horace Mann turned aside from his educational work in 1848 to succeed John Quincy Adams as a Member of Congress. However, Mann's nature was too intense, his animosity too readily aroused to permit him to make for himself a secure place in the national politics of his day. He made a few fast friends, but he made many bitter enemies. Unable to tolerate the usual tricks of politicians, he hewed to the line of harsh reasonableness and let the chips fall where they might. True, he had shown unexpected political strength in his re-election as an independent, despite the most strenuous opposition of Webster, then Secretary of State. But in Washington he was lonely away from his wife and sons, and he grew increasingly weary of the attrition of congressional life. He concluded not to ask to be returned to Congress and declined the Free-Soil nomination for the governorship of Massachusetts. At this time of turning into a new path, he made one of the strangest decisions of his whole life—he agreed to accept the presidency of Antioch College, the cornerstone of which had not yet been laid (June, 1852).

It is strange that Mann should have even considered accepting the Antioch offer. His fame as an educator was world-wide, and his published works were known in most European countries. For his rehabilitation of the common schools of Massachusetts he had received the honorary degree of Doctor of Laws from Harvard (1849) and from Brown, his alma mater. That the Antioch Committee on the Faculty felt enough assurance to offer the presidency to the leading American educator showed supreme confidence in dreams and a total lack of apprehension of what was to follow. A month after Merrifield had begun the construction of Antioch Hall and at a time when less than $50,000 had been raised, Mann was offered a free hand in the development of a non-sectarian, coeducational college in a new country—and promised freedom from financial worries! His own salary as president had been set at $3,000 a year, a sum he might surely have expected to treble at law or lecturing. Also, going to the then remote West meant severing ties of love, friendship, and cultural communion, and foregoing a relatively civilized environment in which his children might be educated. But he was fifty-six years old, and for twenty years he had carefully nurtured a martyr complex which scorned comfort and barely countenanced convenience. When the committee informed him that because of the high cost of building his salary had been reduced to $2,000, he acquiesced without a moment's hesitation, saying he would give the college even better service to make up for the reduction. By the time he arrived on the campus, the salary had been further reduced to $1,500—and this was paid only in part. Later he stated that he had lost thousands of dollars by neglecting his own affairs in order to be faithful to his college duties.

As one who sees undimmed dreams, as one who had caught a glimpse of the Grail, Mann took up the work of the new college with youthful vigor. Part of his furniture and books were lost in transit from the East. Because the President's Mansion was not ready, he and his family lived in a few of the small rooms in North Hall and ate at the commons table with the students. The crudeness of the surroundings and the gaucherie of Western youth were appalling. When he was asked by a fastidious Eastern visitor how and why he tolerated such primitive conditions, he replied, "I can endure anything for the sake of these young people."

The founders of the college had declared for coeducation, and it was tacitly agreed that the new institution should also be non-sectarian. In addition, Mann insisted that the moral tone should be the highest, declaring that knowledge should never be wedded to iniquity, and refusing to grant a diploma to anyone on whose character there was the slightest smirch. He opposed emulation and the awarding of prizes, urging that competition should take the form of self-improvement and that education in itself should be worthy as the highest goal. He favored the admission of Negroes and stood firm when the president of the Board of Trustees, Judge Aaron Harlan, resigned in protest at the admission of the first Negro. He believed that the health of the body was equal in importance with mental and moral health and sought to stamp out bad health habits. He planned the curriculum after that of Harvard and maintained a high academic standard. Antioch under Mann was a financial failure, but over that part of the college administration he had no control.

As a condition of accepting the presidency, Mann had asked

to be allowed to appoint two members of the faculty, so that he might not be surrounded by teachers ignorant of his methods. For these positions he chose his nephew and niece—Calvin Pennell, a graduate of Colby, and Rebecca Pennell, of the West Newton Normal School. The trustees appointed four other instructors—Rev. Thomas Holmes, an alumnus of Oberlin; Rev. Ira W. Allen, a graduate of Union College; Rev. W. H. Doherty, of the Royal Belfast College; and Rev. A. L. McKinney, a son of Wabash. These choices were, on the whole, not very happy ones, for these young men had little to offer the community except the bright precision of the recently graduated. After two years, Holmes resigned to do graduate work in Germany, and McKinney left to re-enter the ministry. Four years later Allen and Doherty were forced out because they opposed Mann's religious tolerance. They were replaced by less brittle minds, but in none of these early instructors, except possibly in Austin Craig and George Cary (later president of Meadville), did Mann find much compatibility. In a letter to Rev. Orin J. Wait, later to follow him as president, Mann commented on his spiritual and cultural isolation in Yellow Springs. Charles Sumner declared that Mann never should have left Massachusetts. The president found some solace in the many addresses he gave before educational groups in Ohio and neighboring states—for which he was roundly denounced on the ground that he was neglecting Antioch. So strong was the feeling against the Unitarians at one time when Theodore Parker came to speak in chapel that Mann asked him not to do so. The villagers and even most of the trustees made evident their distrust of Mann's liberal views, bringing him to exclaim that he was living "among people with souls so small that a million sprinkled on a diamond would not make it dusty!" For thirty years after Mann's death, Antioch might have attracted the most capable teachers in America and might have become in reality the Little Harvard of the West had not this same smallness of soul caused religious quarrels which deflected both men and money elsewhere.

The president labored long hours every day to keep the college open and at its appointed task. Although his own salary was not always paid, he willingly spent his own funds to bring in now and then a well-known speaker, or to print circulars advertising the college, or even to pay postage on the college mail. He was in demand as a lecturer, and his fees usually found their way sooner or later into the college coffers. He loaned money to deserving students to provide proper food and clothing. He had the enthusiastic support of the students, and when he returned to the college after an absence and walked into chapel—tall, erect, gaunt, vibrant—the students rose and cheered and cheered until he stopped them. On one such occasion, when he had been seeking money for the college, he declared that he would not have rejoiced half as much had he found the basement full of gold, badly as the college needed it, as he did to find that no infraction of the moral laws had been reported during his absence.

Although it had been assured he would have no financial worries, it became evident that the college had been insolvent on the day it opened. Most of the students were enrolled on scholarships, supposedly worth $6 a year to the college, and the others paid $8 tuition. Board and room were priced so low they yielded no income. The scholarship money and the endowment, together not more than $50,000, had been spent on the buildings. Friends of the college, notably Peter Cooper, H. W. Bellows, and Moses Grinnell of New York, and Albert Fearing of Boston, helped with gifts of money, but the institution sank rapidly into debt. The otherworldliness of the Christians is evident in their plan to operate a first-class college with an enrollment of 300 and a faculty of nine on an annual income of $6,000!

At the trustee meeting on March 7, 1855, it was found that the college owed $75,000. Under the state law the scholarship holders were responsible for the debt—and in their hysteria they blamed Mann for the whole collapse. By November the college debt had grown to $85,000, and was increasing at the rate of

$1,000 a month, in part due to the excessive interest rate (12%) then allowable in Ohio.

On January 30, 1856, the "Friends of Antioch" met in Hope Chapel, New York City, and pledged $110,000, to be paid by the end of the year—and Antioch was saved "beyond a contingency!" But the hope was false; the pledges were not paid. Matters drifted along until June 26, 1857, when the outgoing Board of Trustees voted to cut off all rights of the scholarship holders, to discharge the faculty, and to assign the college property to satisfy debts against the institution. Suits at law—seventy in New York and four hundred in Ohio—were brought to collect on scholarship notes, and $3,600 was paid in.

The incoming Board of Trustees met on June 30, re-elected Mann, and decided to keep the college open, pledging $3,000 toward expenses. Tuition was raised to $24 a year. In October a convention meeting in Franklin, Ohio, voted to form a joint stock company and raise enough money to pay the college debts, but this came to nothing. A similar meeting in Stafford, N.Y., the following March also failed to furnish the solution.

In the spring of 1858 the debt against the college stood at $83,000. Despite the current money panic, friends in New York City offered to loan $30,000—in reality meant as a gift—if the Christians in New England would pay the so-called Hartford claim of $27,000, and if Ohio Christians would meet the Reyburn claim of $20,000. Judge William Mills, whose fortune had largely disappeared in the collapse of the Yellow Springs real estate bubble, misunderstood the New York offer as a move treacherous to Ohio friends of the college, and bitterly attacked both Mann and the Eastern friends, causing the withdrawal of the loan offer early in June. The outlook seemed again hopeless, but in this dark hour Mrs. A. S. Dean (Miss Pennell) went to New York and after long days of explanation brought about a renewal of the offer. There was, however, still deep despair in Yellow Springs over the necessity of raising $20,000.

When he saw that little if anything was forthcoming, Mann

himself stepped forward and pledged $5,000. He was followed by Charles Ridgway, a trustee ("he of herculean frame and soul"), who pledged all he had in the world, $1,000. A group of others, including E. W. Devore and John Phillips, trustees, and Peter Devore, agreed to contribute $10,000 more. There still remained $4,000. After some time Rev. T. M. McWhinney, a trustee, pledged all his property for $2,000. And then Rev. Eli Fay, Christian minister in Yellow Springs and a favorite of Mann, pledged everything he had to make the remaining $2,000. All these pledges were paid in and the Reyburn claim was satisfied.

The New England Christians failed, however, to pay the Hartford claim. It was decided to allow the property to be foreclosed and to buy it back at the lowest possible price. The assessed value was $60,000, and it could be sold for $40,000. On April 19, 1859, the property was bought at public auction in Cincinnati for Francis A. Palmer of New York City, long a friend of the college, at the minimum price without an opposing bid. The college was transferred to five provisional trustees and on April 22 was placed in the hands of a new Board of Trustees and granted a charter which prohibited debt of any kind and forbade carrying a deficit from one year to the next.

Mann had written to Austin Craig in September, 1856, and again in August, 1857, saying he did not expect to remain much longer president of Antioch. He stuck by the ship, however. The strain of the reorganization in the spring of 1859 had fallen largely upon him. To him fell much of the teaching also, as some of the instructors left to accept other positions. Mann's health, always delicate, had now reached a thin edge. He could neither eat nor sleep, and he wished only to be relieved of the intolerable burden of Antioch. He wrote to the trustees, offering his resignation to take effect at once. At the meeting of the trustees on June 28, a committee was appointed "to wait upon Mr. Mann, and to inform him that he is the first and only choice" for president. Perhaps thinking that a long rest during the summer would make him fit again, Mann relented and was unanimously re-elected.

Commencement day was upon him, and he was expected to do everything. In spite of waning strength he tried to meet every demand. So pressed was he for time that he did not finish writing his Baccalaureate Address until a few minutes before he began to speak. He scarcely had strength to deliver the long address, but his indomitable spirit shone through the words he uttered to inspire those present for many years to come. We still find a measure of his life in the closing sentence, the last he was to speak publicly—"I beseech you to treasure up in your hearts these my parting words: Be ashamed to die until you have won some victory for humanity."

The two-hour commencement dinner was followed in the evening by an equally long and arduous reception by the president. And then came meeting after meeting for three more days. Stifling summer heat lay over the countryside, and there was no relief anywhere. At last the throng departed, thinking to leave him in peace. But he could not rest. A bright flame seared his eyeballs and consumed his brain, and nothing could slake his thirst. Moment by moment he was dying, crucified through his fidelity to Antioch. At last on the morning of August 2 he was told the end was near. He asked to see the students then at the college, and spoke a word of encouragement to each. He promised one to whom he had loaned money that Mrs. Mann would return the note. He spoke calmly to friends and relatives. At 4:30 in the afternoon he died. Later, in a gentle rain, his body was buried on the campus, near the mound on which stands the monument erected to his memory. But even in death he was an alien in a strange land, and a year later his body was reinterred in the North Burial Ground, Providence.

Friends raised $20,000 for his family, and resolutions commemorating his work were passed by scores of meetings. In 1865 his statue was erected in the State House grounds in Boston, opposite that of his former friend and foe, Daniel Webster. There they stand today, two noble sons of Massachusetts—the Great Thunderer and the Father of the Common Schools.

4

Romance Pathetique

ADA SHEPARD AND HENRY BADGER

Among the sophomores who registered at Antioch in September, 1854, were Ada Adaline Shepard, a girl of nineteen from Dorchester, Massachusetts, and Henry Clay Badger, a youth of twenty-one from Honeoye Falls, New York. They went through college together, and for the next twenty years shared some happiness and more misfortune.

Ada was the eldest of five sisters, all charming, lovely, and intelligent. They grew up in a liberal atmosphere in Dorchester and seemed to have been much more sensible than most educated women of their time. They did not succumb to transcendentalism, they did not come under the spell of Margaret Fuller; instead they listened eagerly to Emerson and Theodore Parker and fostered in their minds an independent and inquiring spirit. One of the sisters, Eliza, married Rafael Pumpelly, the geologist; two younger sisters, Lucy and Rebecca, also attended Antioch, and later Lucy married Dr. Thomas Hill, President of Harvard, and Rebecca became the wife of George Haven Putnam, the well-known American publisher.

Henry was the son of Joseph Badger, a minister of the Christian Connexion, who had found the Baptism of New England too restrictive and had broken away and become an independent clergyman. After preaching widely in New England, Eastern Canada, and New York, he had settled in Honeoye Falls. He was one of the first among Christian Ministers to interest himself in founding Antioch and is credited with having chosen the name of the new institution. Early in 1852 he had heard Horace Mann deliver in Rochester a lecture on the Rights and Duties of Women; it was he who urged that Antioch should be coeducational, and he first suggested that the presidency should be offered to Mann. Although Badger found Fundamentalism unsatisfactory, he never quite cleared his own mind of Calvinism and remained somewhat hampered by creedal limitations. For several years he edited the leading denominational magazine, and for a time lectured at Meadville. He died in 1852, before Antioch had opened its doors.

In religious matters Henry was very much like his father. He had the ministry in view and had spent his twentieth year at Amherst. During the summer of 1854 he applied to Eli Fay, representative of the college in New York, for a part-time teaching job in the Preparatory School, and Fay recommended him to Mann as having few equals in the world. He was indeed intelligent and a serious student—a shade too serious, for he had developed introspective habits and was inclined to solitary ways. At Antioch he developed a strong friendship with Cyrus Christie; the two of them boarded with an elderly lady in a farmhouse outside the village and kept much to themselves. For his last year Badger considered transferring to Harvard largely because of the, to him, comparative value of a degree from Harvard and from what he called "this woman's rights seminary." However, he remained, and during his senior year he and Christie returned to the college commons and took more part in student affairs. It was perhaps then that Henry became more aware of the lovely Miss Shepard; he was soon in love with her, and by commencement time they were engaged.

Ada had at once shown herself a superior student and soon became a favorite of President and Mrs. Mann. She had a flair for modern languages and took all the work she could in French, German, and Italian. She was frequently in the Mann home where she was loved almost as a daughter. She had borrowed money to continue in college; her modest blue dress was so long worn that it became associated with her. Her fellow-students themselves dressed modestly, for none of them had money for anything except necessities.

The picture of the graduating class of 1857 shows Ada as a rather small girl, her well-formed oval face framed in long blonde curls. Henry was tall and slender, his hair and beard very black; his later pictures show a close resemblance to the face of Carlyle.

The first class to graduate from Antioch received its diplomas on Wednesday, July 1, 1857. The occasion was a notable one and was reported for the press by Whitelaw Reid, later editor and owner of the New York *Tribune* and minister to France and England. Salmon P. Chase, then governor of Ohio, sat on the platform and declared to President Mann that the exercises surpassed anything he had ever seen in Ohio. The venerable Dr. Gannett of Boston's Arlington Street Church was also on the platform, as was Father Taylor of the Seamen's Bethel in Boston's North End. Many other well-known persons were present, and the Large Chapel was filled.

Ada appeared third on the program, reading her essay, "All Success Proves Partial Failure," and thus probably became the first woman graduate of a coeducational college to read her own essay from the platform on commencement day. In his account of the occasion, Reid said:

> Miss Shepard's essay was one of unusual beauty, one to which a hasty abstract would necessarily do great injustice. The fair author, thoroughly accomplished in all departments of college lore, is perfectly unassuming and modest in her deportment, and it is not strange that the students of Antioch should express their pride in her intellectual successes, which seem to be more than partial. We understand that Miss Shepard is to become for a time a member of the family of Hon. Nathaniel Hawthorne, United States Consul to Liverpool, and who is widely known as the author of *The Scarlet Letter*. The Hawthornes will spend the coming winter in Italy.

The fifteen members of the graduating class had read their parts to each other, resorting to the woods in the Glen for this purpose; each seemed as much interested in the others' success as in his own. Henry appeared near the end of the exercises, reading an original poem. President Mann's address set forth his belief that graduation from college should imply not only some degree of intellectual development but also unimpeachable moral character. Dr. Gannett declared that Mann's address placed Antioch ahead of all other colleges in the country and that the principle, when applied, would be the greatest possible boon to America. Badger observed that "the exacting severity of Mann's moral demands made him seem, as he stood before his pupils, something like the incarnate justice of God."

Three days after commencement, Mann wrote to his friend, Dr. Howe: "We had a good dinner and fun for three hours, which flapped all diaphragms and ventilated the respiratory apparatus very thoroughly."

President Mann had offered Henry the professorship of Logic and Belles-Lettres, and Ada that of Modern Languages. Henry, however, had decided to spend the next year in the Divinity School at Harvard, and Ada, recommended without reservation by the Manns to Mrs. Mann's sister, Mrs. Sophia Hawthorne, had decided to join the Hawthornes in Europe.

In July, 1857, Hawthorne resigned his post as consul at Liverpool and took his family for a tour of Scotland. He had held the consulship for four years under his friend, President Pierce, but the post went to someone else when Buchanan came into office. In September the Hawthornes were settled in Lansdowne Circus, Leamington. Julian Hawthorne has written of this time:

> It was in this place that we were joined by Miss Ada Shepard, who acted as governess in the family during the ensuing two years, and who was at all events a young lady of sound and varied accomplishments, which were yet less noticeable than her winning manners and pleasant aspect. This American girl of three-and-twenty added not a little to the pleasure of our Italian tour, and was invaluable as an interpreter of the various strange tongues one meets with on the Continent.

Una, the elder daughter, was then thirteen, Julian was eleven, and Rose was six. It was Ada's task to teach the children French and Italian, history and English.

On November 10th, the Hawthornes went to London and there lodged in Great Russell Street. Their plans to proceed to Rome were held up while the children recovered from the measles. On January 3, 1858, a gloomy, wintry day, they left London by train for Folkestone and crossed the Channel. The crossing was very rough, for the time dulling Sophia's radiant smile and prostrating the amiable and philosophic Ada. Julian records that when they had reached Boulogne,

> Miss Shephard, now restored to life, made amends for her late incompetence by discoursing with excited French officials with what seemed to me preternatural intelligence; indeed, I half doubted whether

there was not some conspiracy in that torrent of outlandish sounds which she and they were so rapidly pouring forth to one another. However, all turned out well.

On January 5 they reached Paris and rested for a week. On the 12th they departed for Lyons where they spent the night, then went on to Marseilles. After two days in this bleak and windy city, they embarked for Civita Vecchia, stopping on the way at Genoa and Leghorn. From Civita Vecchia they traveled by vettura at night, over roads infested with brigands, and arrived at Rome near midnight in a cold, sleety rain. A few days later they were settled in Palazzo Larazani in Via Porta Pinciana.

They had arrive in Rome just in time for the February carnival, and all entered into the spirit of the occasion. All of the family enjoyed walks through the city. Sophia and Una were busy sketching, Ada and the children were busy with lessons, and Hawthorne renewed his acquaintance with William Story, the American sculptor, and was deep in the writing of his new novel, *The Marble Faun*.

On May 24th the Hawthornes left by vettura for Florence. The ten-day journey through the beautiful region was broken by stops at small inns. Sophia reported to her mother that the journey had been one of the brightest and most carefree interludes imaginable. In Florence they found lodgings in the Casa del Bello; the Brownings lived near-by in the Casa Guida, and Hiram Powers' studio was close by. About August 1st they moved to Villa Manteuto, where they remained until their return to Rome at the beginning of October. Hawthorne worked away at his book through the hot summer months.

While they were in Florence they had frequent visits with the Brownings. Julian reports:

> At the instance of Mrs. Browning, who was often with us, we held spirit seances, Miss Shepard being medium, though she mildly protested. Long communications were written down in various handwritings all unlike her own, but the skeptics were not converted, nor were the believers discouraged.

Both Hawthorne and Browning disliked this occultism, and, with Miss Shepard herself, made light of it, explaining that it was merely telepathy. Hawthorne wrote: "Her integrity is absolutely indubitable, and she herself disbelieves in the spiritual authenticity of what is communicated through her medium." Sophia and Mrs. Browning were somewhat inclined to believe the messages authentic. Many years later Browning could not remember that he had ever been present at one of Ada's seances.

The Hawthornes left Florence October 1, 1858, traveling by train to Siena, where they remained ten days; then they went on by vettura, reaching Rome five days later. They put up in Piazza Poli, and remained there six months. Soon after their arrival in Rome, Una worked too hard at sketching and remained late one evening to finish a drawing of the Palace of the Caesars; she came down with Roman fever and was very ill for some time, and never fully recovered. The family was kept somewhat at home caring for the patient and spent evenings at whist, euchre, and old maid. Among their American friends who visited them in Rome were Ex-President Pierce, Senator Sumner, and John Lothrop Motley. By the time of the spring carnival, Una had recovered sufficiently to take drives. One day while she and her father were riding in an open barouche through the crowded streets, the Prince of Wales (Edward VII), recognizing Hawthorne, stepped forward and presented two bouquets to Una.

In Rome Julian sometimes arose at five to watch the sun rise over the dome of St. Peter's or St. Angelo's. He writes

I painted my experiences in colors so attractive that Miss Shepard was inflamed with the idea of accompanying me on my rambles. She was a child at heart, though so mature in intellect, and her spirit so valiant though her flesh was comparatively infirm. She promised to be ready at five. But after keeping awake most of the night in order not to fail of the appointment, she fell asleep and dreamed only of getting up; and, after waiting for her for near an hour, I went without her. She was much mortified at her failure, and suggested a plan to insure her punctuality, in which I readily agreed to collaborate. When she went to bed she attached a piece of string to one of her toes, the other end being carried underneath doors and along passages to my own room. I was instructed to haul in on my slack at the proper hour, and this I accordingly did, with good-will, and was at once made conscious that I had caught something, not only by the resistance which my efforts encountered, but by the cries of feminine distress and supplication heard in the distance. However, my companion appeared in due season, and we took our walk, which, she declared, fulfilled all the anticipations which my reports had led her to form.

Julian writes further: "My mother and sister sketched continually, and Miss Shepard was always ready to tell us the story of the historical features which we encountered; it astonished me to note how much she knew about things she had never seen before." While she was in Rome, Ada, deeply interested in original sources, had a long conference with Cardinal Newman over the Codex Sinai.

On May 26, 1859, the Hawthornes left Rome for Civita Vecchia, then they went on by boat to Marseilles. Traveling slowly by way of Avignon, they arrived at Geneva on June 7th and spent a week there. Julian writes:

After leaving Chillon and Geneva, our faces were turned homeward, and we hastened our steps. We returned to Paris, and after a few days there proceeded to Havre, in order to see Miss Shepard safe on board her steamer for home; her *Wanderjahr* was over, and she was now to be married to Henry Clay Badger. We were sorry to say good-bye to her; she had been a faithful and valuable element in our household, and she had become a dear friend and comrade. She stood waving her handkerchief to us as her steamer slipped away down the harbor. She, too, was sorry for the parting. She once had said to me, "I think your father is the wisest man I ever knew; he does not seem ever to say much, but what he does say is always the truest and best thing that could be said."

The Hawthornes went through London to Whitby on the Yorkshire coast, and there, at Red Cedar, Hawthorne worked away at *The Marble Faun*. The book was published in London three months later. There has been some question whether either

Sophia or Ada served as prototype for Hilda in this book. Sophia declared that any resemblance to herself was accidental. Julian believed that the character of Hilda was an abstraction and bore not the slightest trace of either his mother or the governess. Hawthorne's friend and biographer, Moncure Conway, was of the opinion that Hilda represented the feminine counterpart of Hawthornes's own character and therefore was not based on either Sophia or Ada. Nevertheless, Hilda does resemble both. Hawthorne was consistently silent about such similarities; he never admitted that he had fashioned Zenobia in *The Blithedale Romance* after Margaret Fuller, but this he clearly did.

The Hawthornes had intended to return to America about August 1st but, finding themselves comfortable in Yorkshire, decided to stay on. In the meantime Mann had died in Yellow Springs, and Mrs. Mann and her sons went to Concord to occupy the Hawthorne house. After the Hawthornes returned in June, 1860, the Manns moved to their own house near Emerson's in the eastern part of the village.

While Ada was in Europe, letters passed regularly between her and Henry. They made a game of looking at a certain star, at the same time each thinking of the other. It is probable that Henry thought little of any other girl, but romantics will forever speculate on the resemblance between Ada and Hilda, and wonder whether Ada was not more or less in love with a sculptor in Rome. Be that as it may, she returned to Dorchester early in July, 1859, looking forward to her marriage and taking up her work as Professor of Modern Languages. Both Ada and Henry were deeply affected by the death of President Mann in August. Ada wrote an affectionate letter to Mrs. Mann, expressing her love for her teacher and the pleasure with which she had expected to work under him at Antioch. Henry had become a member of the faculty in the fall of 1858. He was deeply distressed during the President's last illness and had visited Mann a short time before his death. The President had placed his faltering hand upon Badger's head, had expressed his admiration of Henry's ability, and had urged him to guard against the disintegrating forces which might balk or counteract his usefulness.

In September the young professors, now married, took up their tasks as members of the faculty. They greatly missed their friends in the President's Mansion, now empty and deserted. Henry planted a willow near Mann's grave on the campus; he wrote to Mrs. Mann about conditions at the college, deploring the increasing giddiness of the girls and the greater uncouthness of the men. At first the Badgers lived in a small house at the corner of Limestone and President Streets; later they moved to a small brick gardener's cottage on the Mills Lawn. Ada was very popular as a teacher, and Henry only a little less so. When the alumni met for the first time and organized the Alumni Association on June 26, 1861, Ada was elected secretary.

When President Hill resigned in the spring of 1862 and the faculty dispersed, Henry decided to join the Union army. For some time he and Professor Bardwell had been officers of the Antioch Cadets, had drilled the boys on the campus and in the Large Chapel, and had proudly lined them up near the depot in Xenia to be reviewed by President-elect Lincoln, on his way to Washington to be inaugurated.

When Ada realized that her husband was determined to join the army, she arranged with Dr. Bellows to give them both posts in the Sanitary Commission, the Red Cross of that day. They folllowed the Army of the Potomac as it moved through Virginia and were present at the battles fought during the campaign of 1862-63. Engaged in her work of mercy on the battlefield of Antietam, Ada came upon a dying boy in blue; the soldier recognized her and called to her. He was a young student who had been in one of her classes in the Antioch Preparatory School; he died in her arms. Soon after this Ada returned to the old Shepard home in Dorchester, and Henry was sent by Dr. Bellows to assist his old friend, Cyrus Christie, then in charge of the work of the Sanitary Commission at Memphis.

In 1864 Dr. Bellows asked Badger to accompany him to San

Francisco, to fill temporarily the pulpit left vacant by the death of Starr King. It may be assumed that Bellows planned to install Badger in the pastorate, but Henry seems not to have liked the prospect. One day while he was riding horseback, Henry fell insensible from his mount. He sometimes fainted when under stress or when he suffered a shock.

Henry returned to Cambridge, and there in 1865 he was ordained in the Unitarian ministry by President Hill and Edward Everett Hale. The Badgers lived for many years in the old Washington Allston mansion in Cambridgeport; there their four children passed their infancy. Henry's health grew gradually worse, and finally he suffered a breakdown which incapacitated him for several months. Ada, ever resourceful, started a school for girls in a house in Springfield Street, Boston, and it soon became a flourishing institution. After Henry had recovered his health, he assumed the pastorate of Christ Church in Dorchester, and Ada continued with her school. Not long afterward, she was elected to the Boston School Board.

Before her marriage Ada had belonged to no church; her mind was too independent to be bound by creeds. Henry, however, was inclined to conformity. When after many years she told him that she had lost her belief in immortality, he fell insensible; thereafter he believed her reason to be in danger, and she, acutely sensitive, came to believe that his misfortunes were due to her lack of faith. After a time she confessed to him her belief that she was becoming insane, and he too thought that the same derangement might be coming to him. They promised each other that should one of them lose his reason, the other would not have the afflicted one committed to an institution. So the abnormal tension grew and the shadow gathered, as they both brooded over the possibility.

Henry had asked their friend, a Miss Abbott, to spend a week-end in the Badger home in order that she might observe Ada. As he left the house Sunday morning for his church in Dorchester, he slipped under Miss Abbott's door a note giving the address of a physician to be called if necessary; he was not aware that Ada on the landing above had seen him do this. She was convinced that they thought her insane; she returned to her room and made preparations for her departure. She left the affairs of the school in perfect order; she wrote a letter to her husband telling him not to look for her because he would never find her. As she was leaving the house, she met him at the front door; she said she was going to make a call, and he did not know that anything was wrong. When she failed to return after a time, he went to her room and there found the letter. Reading it, he fell insensible, for he knew quite well what she planned to do. She had once told him that when she died she wished it would be off the Point Judith lighthouse at the western entrance to Narragansett Bay. He knew that she planned to take the Fall River boat for New York, and would jump off the boat at Point Judith.

He rushed to the telegraph office and sent wires to Fall River and Newport, asking that Ada be detained. He then engaged a railway engine and rushed to Fall River as fast as steam could carry him. There he found that the wire had not arrived until after the boat had sailed. There was still the chance of intercepting her at Newport, and again he drove the engine at full speed. When he arrived he learned that the boat was not scheduled to stop at Newport. Realizing at last that he could do nothing to prevent Ada's suicide, he fell insensible. Later he sent a telegram to his brother in New York, asking him to meet the Fall River boat. The brother did so and found in Ada's stateroom a farewell letter to her sons, asking their forgiveness and urging them to do the best they could without her. Henry was never to find her again. At the age of thirty-nine, to avoid the darkness and helplessness of insanity, she had drowned herself.

During the remaining years of his life, Henry was a man burdened with grief for his dead wife. For some years he was in charge of the map department of the Harvard library. In June, 1890, still handsome and impressive, he spoke before the literary societies at the college on "Our Antioch Ideals." He recalled his experiences under Mann in the early days of the college; he declared that Mann had had a clear conception of spiritual things, that his ideal was noble, true, and high, that the mind should be trained along with morals and manners, will and instinct, heart and soul. He ended with this peroration:

> Show me another school in the world whose pupils were gathered from so wide an area, from so many States, which yet had such unity and such purity of life. Show me one that had within its walls so little vice. Show me one where women were held in higher honor. Show me one whose alumni were so largely teachers. Show me one that had, from the dawn of her day, so fair an ideal of home-life, so sweet an ideal of Christ the Lord, or so high an ideal of what scholarship, womanhood, and Christian manhood should be. These ideals, these dreams have walked incarnate here!

Four years later, at the age of sixty-one, he too was dead.

5

A Man of Many Talents

PRESIDENT THOMAS HILL

Walking one afternoon with the dignified Professor Torrey, President Hill of Harvard College paused and without ceremony removed one of his oxfords and therefrom removed a pebble, within sight of the whole college yard. This commonplace occurrence so outraged Professor Torrey that thereafter he steadfastly refused to walk with Dr. Hill again. And the other

Brahmins of the Charles shared an unmitigated grief that a man so lacking in the fussiness that then passed for culture—and incidentally so lacking in family coats-of-arms—had ever been elevated to the presidency of America's oldest college. A combination of strong opponents and ill-fortune forced his resignation after a tenancy of only five and a half years, and he was soon forgotten. As a former president of Antioch, he was remembered in Yellow Springs as long as he lived and indeed is still remembered, but so completely had he been forgotten in Cambridge in 1886, when he attended the two hundred and fiftieth anniversary of the founding of Harvard, sixteen years after he had been succeeded by Charles W. Eliot, he appeared not as the only living ex-president but as a member of the class of 1843.

One of Dr. Hill's biographers says of him that "he was admired by the scientists for his theology and by the theologians for his science." Perhaps more of the admiration came from the scientists, however, and not without reason, for his unusual and versatile talents in science, mathematics, and the fine arts brought him sincere admiration from such men as Agassiz and Peirce, while his work in the pulpit was perhaps less satisfactory even to himself. To the last day of his life he seems not to have regretted choosing the ministry and indeed was one of the pioneers in America who sought to reconcile science and religion.

The son of a father from Warwick and of a mother from Cambridgeshire, Thomas Hill was born in New Brunswick, N.J., January 7, 1818. The parents, both Unitarians, had come to America to escape religious restrictions. The father encouraged the boy's great interest in plants and patiently taught him as much botany as he could. When he was six his mother died, and when he was ten his father too was dead, and he was left to the care of his older brothers. Apprenticed to a printer when he was twelve, he learned to set type and spent the few leisure hours at his command reading the works of Benjamin Franklin and Erasmus Darwin. After a time, however, he found the bad food no longer bearable and so ran away, having decided to live with the Cherokee Indians. Thirty-six hours of hitch-hiking proved to be wasted, for he was found and returned to the printer, who, not to be outdone, refused to take him back. Thomas then attended school for several months. At fifteen he was again apprenticed, this time to an apothecary, and remained until he was twenty. During this time he spent his free time studying botany and collecting plants.

At the age of nineteen he decided he wanted to enter the ministry and, with the approval of his brothers, set about making plans to enter the Harvard Divinity School. In May, 1838, he began his preparation under Dr. Stebbins at Leominster who taught him Greek, Latin, and Hebrew—and he continued botany on his own. After a few months he rounded out his preparation for Harvard at the Leicester Academy.

In 1839, at the age of twenty-one, he entered Harvard College, one of seventy freshmen. He was assigned a room in Hollis Hall, but during a severe bout of hazing the windows of his room were wrecked, and he moved to Massachusetts Hall. During vacations he set type and taught school. Early he came to the attention of Professor Benjamin Peirce, and that masterly scholar gave his best to this lad who was undoubtedly a genius in mathematics. They took frequent walks together. It was not unusual to see the teacher and his pupil standing in deep conversation, the student attentive while the professor drew figures in the dust with his boot. They worked together at the meteorological station and spent many hours together over their problems.

During his last year as an undergraduate he was permitted to take the first year's work in the Divinity School, for much as he was drawn toward science, and despite Dr. Peirce's urging that he devote himself to mathematics, he clung to his intention of becoming a minister. It is likely that he would have become one of the great mathematicians of his time. During his senior year he invented the "occulator," a device for calculating the times and paths of eclipses, and for this invention received the

Scott medal from the Franklin Society. Upon his graduation he was offered the directorship of the National Observatory in Washington, at the suggestion of Professor Peirce, but this he declined. In this year he published his first volume of verse, *Christmas and Poems on Slavery*.

He was graduated from the Harvard Divinity School in 1845, and on Thanksgiving Day of that year was married to Anne Foster Bellows of Walpole, N.H., a woman of rare beauty, character, and ability, whom he had met through her cousins, his classmates in Harvard College. In December he assumed the pastorate of the Unitarian Society in Waltham, a post he retained for fourteen years. In the same year he published *An Elementary Treatise on Arithmetic*, which Professor Peirce made a standard entrance requirement to Harvard.

His years at Waltham were the happiest of his life and perhaps among the most useful. One son and four daughters were born and found the Reverend Thomas Hill a most delightful and satisfactory father. These children were privileged indeed, for among the frequent visitors at the Hill home were Peirce and Agassiz. In the Swiss master especially they recognized a marvellously lugubrious playmate. Peirce came to Hill with mathematical inspirations for clarifications and conclusions, and Agassiz came for companionship and help in collecting specimens.

In 1849 appeared his *Geometry and Faith* in which he restated his belief that science was a constant unfolding of the law and wisdom of God. He gave the Phi Beta Kappa oration at Harvard, "Liberal Education," in 1858. During these years many of his papers appeared in the journals devoted to astronomy, mathematics, and religion. He invented a "ready reckoner," a machine for adding and subtracting, and developed a process for electroplating. He was offered the presidency of the Meadville Theological School in 1855 but declined, saying he was much attached to Waltham and preferred to stay there. He was a member of the Waltham School Board during the fourteen years of his residence there, serving as chairman most of the time. He would have found much more contentment in life if he had remained minister of that First Church in Waltham.

From the time of the establishment of Antioch he had been deeply interested, both because of his own concern with education and his admiration for President Mann and because of the great enthusiasm for Antioch shown by his wife's cousin, Dr. Henry W. Bellows of New York, a trustee of the college. About ten days after the death of Mann, Dr. Bellows visited Hill in Waltham to ask permission to present Hill's name as a candidate for the Antioch presidency. As a liberal minister much interested in education, science, and mathematics, he seemed to be an ideal man for the post. Hill was doubtful of his ability to head the college, but he was reassured on that score by his friends, Dr. Gannett of the Arlington Street Church and President Walker of Harvard, both of whom felt strongly that Hill should assume the task. Hill was dubious too about the college having sufficient income and made it a condition of acceptance that salaries and running expenses must be guaranteed for three years. He was reluctant to undertake the task, and wrote to a friend:

> I most sincerely wish that the Christians at Antioch would utterly refuse to have a Unitarian minister as president. However I dare not hope it. I am afraid that they will formally appoint me and then I suppose I must go. When once I feel there is no escape, I have no doubt that courage and zeal will arise in my heart.

The Antioch trustees met in Yellow Springs on the morning of September 7, 1859. Mr. and Mrs. Hill had come as far as Philadelphia, there to await the telegram from Ohio telling them to come on at once in case the ballot was favorable. The vote proved to be unanimous. On the afternoon of the following day Mr. Hill was inaugurated second president of Antioch, the formal ceremony taking place in the Large Chapel. The subject of his inaugural address was "Integral Education."

The Hills remained in Yellow Springs a fortnight while he conferred with the faculty, heard recitations, and took stock of the situation. They then returned to Waltham, leaving the college in the charge of Professor John Burns Weston. President Hill set about the preparation of a series of lectures on "The Mutual Relation of the Sciences" which he was to deliver in December before the Lowell Institute in Boston.

At about this time he wrote to Dr. Bellows: "Mann has already embodied at Antioch more of my own ideas of education than are embodied anywhere else in Christiandom." And later: "I like all things at Antioch. . . . I feel as though I had entered on a glorious field of labor. Heaven grant I may improve it well, and show myself a workman that needeth not be ashamed."

The Hill family moved to Yellow Springs in January, 1860, and the president took over active management of the college. At first sight of the President's House, he said it would "need a good deal done to it to make it look as we shall like to have it." His nephew, Franklin Hill, came with them and became the handy man who "wedged up the piazza, mended the pump, put the stove to rights, and generally made the place livable."

The new president sought to improve spirit and discipline, and as one means to that end worked untiringly to improve the appearance of the campus and buildings. As the weather became warmer he turned with spade and rake to the college grounds, then little better than a pasture. During the summer vacation some of the students stayed to help mow weeds, repair the walks, and plant shrubs. The improvement was noticed even at the next commencement, when former students spoke of it, and continued with each succeeding year. In November, 1860, he wrote to Bellows:

All goes smoothly, except finances . . . I have moved a great many trees, dug around others, trimmed, smoothed and graveled walks and roads, planted quantities of shrubs and vines, etc., and altogether made the appearance of things more respectable. Then Frank Hill has mended all the broken glass (five hundred panes were out and had been for a long time), built a piazza at the east end of North Hall, mended the cellar doors, etc., of Antioch Hall and stored the wood in the cellar, repaired the settees, etc., in the recitation rooms, and in short "slicked up" and repaired all internals as I have externals.

In the spring of 1862, when war threatened to close the college, Hill wrote back to Waltham: "I have been at work planting shrubs, etc. Antioch ground shall bear my mark for many a long year (unless pigs and cows are allowed to run in next year)." The campus still bears his mark in abundance, for it was President Hill who planted the ivy, trumpet vine, and woodbine on Antioch Hall and the dormitories, the elms which surround the library[1], and many of the trees on the campus. Many trees were planted by students under his direction.

The trustees adopted a plan for paths and roads on the campus, drawn for them by R. Morris Copeland of Boston, but little money was provided for this purpose. Hill wrote to the trustees: "Mud is tremendous here in winter, and I felt that I must make the paths drier next winter. So I have spent the money partly on existing paths, even where not consonant with your plan." The plan was never carried out, for the mud continued to be tremendous and money scarce.

There was no hazing at Antioch, and the president was pleased to find that the students aided instead of opposed the college authorities. Someone said of him at this time that he pursued a course of "holy calmness, expecting the best of everyone," and the best was forthcoming from the students and faculty.

The high level of instruction was maintained, for President Hill was fortunate in his faculty. Greek and Latin were taught by the greatly beloved George Lovell Cary; botany, chemistry, and physics by George Chapman Caldwell; mathematics and engineering by the handsome and shy Frederic Bardwell; history by the benevolent John Burns Weston, '57; modern languages by Ada Shepard Badger, '57; English by Henry Clay Badger, '57; zoology, physiology, and geology by Dr. H. W. Warriner, and

---

[1] The former Horace Mann Library, built in 1925 on the site of Horace Mann's home, which had burned down. When the Olive Kettering Library was built on the other side of the campus (1955), the old Library was remodelled into classroom and office space for the departments of Literature, Languages, and Philosophy, and renamed Mann Hall. Most of the campus elms dating back to President Hill succumbed to blight in the 1940's.—L. F.

music by Louis Fessenden. The president himself was professor of metaphysics, ethics, and natural religion.

Despite his heavy duties at the college, President Hill preached every Sunday at the Church of the Redeemer in Cincinnati, because he loved to preach and because he needed the additional income. He spoke frequently in neighboring cities and often in nearby states, seeking to raise the educational level of the Middle West. In 1860 he published *Jesus, the Interpreter of Nature* and in August of that year received from Harvard the degree of Doctor in Sacred Theology. In the little spare time that was his, he continued his investigations in mathematics; he discovered the curve known as the Tantalus and sought to work out the formulae for the curves he found in leaves and other organic forms. He was an ardent lover of music, and besides his writing of poetry he painted landscapes in oil and modeled portraits in bas-relief. He was indeed a man of many talents.

Although assurances had been given that the expenses of the college would be met, there was not sufficient money to operate the institution even on a cheese-paring basis. The members of the faculty contributed about twenty-five per cent of their already very small salaries, and for months at a time the president received nothing at all. With the approach of the war and the increasingly hard times, the number of students fell off, further impairing the income. In the spring of 1861, Dr. Hill thought of resigning, believing that the failure to supply money for expenses released him from his obligation to the college, but Professor Weston encouraged him to stay by saying "thirteen students under Dr. Hill are better than a hundred without him." Although the president was forced to borrow money for living expenses on his own credit, he yet found a few dollars to help along a few students no longer able to pay their own way. Learning that a good student would have to leave college through lack of funds, he placed a fifty dollar bill in an envelope addressed to her, without any indication of its source, passed it to her through an instructor, and so enabled her to finish her course.

In October, 1861, the president suffered a heart attack but quickly recovered. He took active part in the work of the local branch of the Sanitary Commission by inventing a simple machine for winding the bandages the women of the village were preparing for use on the battlefields.

Hill inherited President Mann's feud with the fundamentalists amoung the Christians, who opposed him chiefly because he was a Unitarian. Those who were more progressive and who helped him in Antioch matters he termed "Christian" Christians. But the stupidity was monumental, and the constant sniping of the disgruntled disturbed him considerably. His enthusiasm for Antioch continued unabated, despite the opposition. In February, 1862, he wrote to Bellows: "My heart is in Antioch. Give me $1,000 per annum (half my nominal salary) and give me reasonable prospect of speedy success and I would stay." Two months later he wrote again:

> With $100,000 invested at 7%, I could do a work here at Antioch second to that done at no other institution in the world, measuring I mean by the usefulness of the results. . . . I told my people at Waltham some nine years ago that the history of America began with the founding of Antioch College, and if I had $100,000 I'd prove that the statement was not extravagant.

Soon after he came to Antioch he had been offered the pastorate of King's Chapel in Boston, and the offer had remained standing. His congregation in Cincinnati wished him to take full charge of the church there. But he preferred to stay at Antioch and remained as long as there was the slightest hope that an adequate endowment could be raised. When there was no longer any hope, he gave up most reluctantly. We may fully agree with his biographer: "Looking back at Antioch one feels that Hill achieved success: that had not the war interrupted he would have become famed in education."

Early in 1862 the resignation of Dr. Walker left the Harvard presidency vacant. Since it was clear that Antioch would be closed for lack of funds, Dr. Bellows, a member of the Harvard

Board of Overseers, joined with Peirce and Agassiz in urging Dr. Hill to allow his name to be put forward for the vacancy. Hill replied from Yellow Springs: "I should prefer staying here to anything else." Early in May, however, he resigned as of July 1, at the same time giving much more serious consideration to the Cincinnati offer than to the Harvard possibility. The Corporation of Harvard met on April 26 and elected Hill president, but three weeks later, after his resignation from Antioch, the Overseers declined to concur, giving as their reason "that Dr. Hill's predilection for the physical and exact sciences would give undue preference to those studies, and that the just claims of polite and classical literature might be slighted." About the middle of June, Hill wrote to Bellows: "An endowment of $100,000 offered to Antioch on condition of my staying, would in the present state of affairs, fix me happily here." He was, however, renamed by the Corporation on September 9, and confirmed by the Overseers on October 6, and on March 24, 1863, he was inaugurated twentieth president of Harvard College. In the same year Yale awarded him the degree of Doctor of Laws.

Essentially a teacher and a theorist in the cause of education, Dr. Hill was not a brilliant president of Harvard and always thought himself a failure in that post. He seems to have been purposely belittled by the Harvard aristocracy; his simplicity was taken for commonness and his gentleness for weakness. Transparently frank and guileless, he was faithful to his duty and just and friendly to everyone. He unwittingly raised many eyebrows in Cambridge by spading like any gardener on the sacred Harvard campus, as he had done at Antioch. He planted ivy, Virginia creeper, and trumpet vine about Gore and Boylston halls and was deeply interested in keeping the grounds neat and tidy. His funds depleted by the lean years at Antioch, he could not have entertained had he wished to do so, and this simplicity of living did not enhance his standing among those who lived by externals.

On one occasion he was obliged to make an address in Latin and, although he had not written a Latin sentence in twenty years, the speech which he prepared was pronounced by Professor Lane to be faultless. And the Overseers had thought that he might slight polite and classical literature!

A genial, gentle man, President Hill suggested but he did not insist. With Peirce, Agassiz, and Asa Grey, he reorganized the Lawrence Scientific School and placed it under Wolcott Gibbs, Rumford Professor of Chemistry. He revived the University Lectures by giving a series himself, and from this renewal grew the university extension system. He originated the Academic Council, from which grew the Graduate School of Arts and Sciences. He suggested that graduate work be permitted and that advanced degrees be awarded for satisfactory work. He thought that the undergraduate course should be broadened by displacing most of the Latin and Greek with science and other more modern subjects. He held that less recitation and more lecturing would be an improvement. He was not greatly disturbed when many parents complained that the courses were too difficult. He revived the elective system, making electives free choices with full credit. During his presidency the Mining and Dental Schools were established, the Sturgis-Hooper Professorship endowed, the Peabody Museum founded, the Bussey Institute set up, and Harvard separated from the control of the state legislature. Under Dr. Hill Harvard "changed from an undergraduate college with appended professional schools to a university which would add to knowledge as well as disseminate it." His successor, Dr. Eliot, said: "I have always been thankful that it was he who had charge of the University for the seven [*sic*] years preceeding my election to the presidency."

In 1864, almost a year after his inauguration, his wife died, leaving five children. His own health had not been good since his Antioch days, and his personal grief as well as the friction and misunderstanding associated with his office worked to discourage him and to hamper his work. In July, 1866, he was married to Miss Lucy Shepard who had studied under him at Antioch and who had been for some time a teacher in the

Cambridge Latin School. She was ideally suited to be his wife. The happiness which came to them both was to be of short duration, however, for in about a year she had become an invalid. The situation became such that Dr. Hill felt he could no longer adequately carry out his duties, and in September, 1868, he resigned. In December a son was born, and in the following February the mother died.

He retired to Waltham to seek rest and the restoration of his health. He traveled here and there, visiting Yellow Springs in March, 1869, on his way to the West Coast over the recently completed Union Pacific. He became interested in the culture of cranberries and developed plantings at Sutton, Mass., and West Creek, N.J. In December, 1870, he again gave the Lowell Lectures, this time on "The National Sources of Theology." For two years he was a member of the Harvard Board of Overseers, and for one term represented Waltham in the state legislature. In December, 1871, he sailed from Boston as botanist, physicist, and photographer with the Hassler Expedition under Agassiz. The expedition sailed around Cape Horn to the Galapagos, reaching San Francisco the following September. In his reports on the expedition he opposed strongly Darwin's theory of accidental variations. In February, 1873, he assumed the pastorate of the Unitarian Church in Portland, Maine, and remained there the rest of his life.

His interest in science, mathematics, and invention continued throughout his life. Questioned once by a skeptic about how he expected to spend eternity, he replied that he would be contented to spend a thousand years on conic sections alone. Many of his scientific articles appeared in print. In 1876 he invented the "nautigon," an instrument for determining longitude and latitude without the use of logarithms. He prepared many religious and theological articles for the more liberal journals. In 1887 appeared a collection of his poems, *In the Woods and Elsewhere*.

During the last ten years of his life he was non-resident Professor of Natural Theology and Ethics at Meadville. In May, 1891, at the age of seventy-three, he set out from Portland for

Meadville, going roundabout to visit Yellow Springs on the way. He spoke in chapel at Antioch one morning and found much pleasure in revisiting old scenes. At Meadville he walked through the woods where he found and identified twenty wild flowers. The strain of the travel and of delivering the lectures so weakened him that he returned to Waltham in failing health. He died at the home of his daughter, Mrs. Alfred Worcester, November 21, 1891.

Although a very capable and learned scholar, Dr. Hill preferred to live on the genial plane of everyday cordiality. In September, 1884, he wrote to his nephew, Franklin Hill:

> I have a story to tell you about a parrot which I saw at Leicester. The anecdote is true. . . . The parrot is known to be thirty-five years old or more. Its present owners, educated and bright people, have had it for many years, and always thought it to be a male bird until two years ago or less; when it suddenly called out—"Bring hot water! Hot water! Quick!" and wriggled and writhed as though in pain. It grew more and more excited, demanding hot water, ginger and camphor in quick succession, and rolling about as if it had a sharp turn of the colic. The family was greatly excited, and afraid he was going to die, when he suddenly laid an egg, and became henceforth —she. She cackled and screamed and exulted greatly over the egg, and henceforth for several weeks laid an egg every day.

6

He Conversed Like an Archangel

DR. AUSTIN CRAIG, PROFESSOR AND PRESIDENT

Characteristically Antiochian perhaps to as great a degree as any professor who ever taught at the college, Dr. Craig would doubtless find considerable satisfaction in the Antioch of the present day. The institution seems to have moved in the direction he would have chosen, we would have found in this modest, gentle, and unassuming parson a surprisingly congenial companion. One of his biographers said of him: "He was extremely independent and individualistic, never disciplining himself to harness of any kind."

In the early 1850's the Reverend Austin Craig was in charge of a liberal parish in Blooming Grove, a rural community in Orange County, New York, a few miles west of the Hudson. He looked upon his pastorate as ideal. In his quiet house amid the rolling hills he found a blessed opportunity to write and study, to watch the seasons change the fields and woods about him, while he gave gentle direction to the youth of his parish and spoke quietly with the elders. To stimulate interest in literary matters, he set up a reading club, and to bring in prominent men from the outside world, he established a lecture society. He took a keen interest in scientific matters and once took a group of his young men to Albany to attend a meeting of the American Association for the Advancement of Science.

Son of a New Jersey teacher and merchant, Craig early turned toward the liberal ministry. Preachers of all faiths and mostly of the sky pilot variety frequently stopped at the Craig home, and the young man was much interested in their discussions. He withdrew from Lafayette College in his junior year because the faculty would not permit him to study the early Christian writers in place of the usual Greek and Latin authors. Later he returned to Lafayette for special work in Hebrew and advanced Greek and was awarded both the bachelor's and the master's degree. He had a most vigorous and retentive mind. It was said of him that he had "a wider and deeper knowledge of the original texts of the Old and New Testaments than that possessed by perhaps any other American of his time." William Cullen Bryant considered him one of the best New Testament Greek scholars in America.

Horace Greeley came to lecture before the group at Blooming Grove and went away with vast admiration for the youthful minister. Greeley had already published in the *Tribune* the address which Craig gave before the New Jersey Christian Conference at Irvington in 1850. In this discourse, which became a state paper of the church, Craig condemned sectarianism and pleaded for

Christian unity. The tone of the paper may be inferred from Craig's words: "From my heart's bottom I hate restrictions upon free inquiry and free discussion."

Henry Ward Beecher also spoke before the lecture club at Blooming Grove and was pleased with the atmosphere of the place. He was perhaps the most popular clergyman in America, yet he said of Craig: "Whenever I have met that man, I have felt like taking a stool and sitting at his feet and listening to his words as long as he would talk to me."

The Blooming Grove pastor had read a small book written by a Massachusetts congressman who had spent many years promoting educational and other reforms. This book was *Thoughts for a Young Man*, and the author was Horace Mann. Craig asked Mann to appear before the lecture society, offering him the usual stipend of $25 and free lodging at the parsonage. Mann accepted and delivered his two lectures on the Rights and Duties of Women, on February 21 and 22, 1852. On the latter date he wrote to Mrs. Mann that he found Craig "a most extraordinary young man. He is very earnest and sincere, has a fine cerebral development, though small in the lungs and in the assimilative organs. I hardly know another such lover of the true." Mann found his room at the parsonage unheated and well ventilated; he swathed himself in blankets but could not sleep because of the intense cold. "It is some compensation, however, to find such a man and such a people. It shows what the people would be if orthodoxy would let them alone." Craig also found much to admire in Mann and was among those who urged the appointment of Mann to the Antioch presidency a few months later.

By August Mann had decided to accept the Antioch offer and wrote Craig pressing him to accept a place on the faculty, with a view to succeeding to the presidency in a few years. Craig felt that his place was at Blooming Grove, and declined. As long as Mann lived he tried to persuade Craig to come to Antioch permanently. Twice Craig did spend a year on the faculty, returning each time to Blooming Grove—he was torn between the desire to answer the pleas of his friend and his own preference for his parish.

In September, 1855, Craig obtained leave of absence from his church and came to Antioch as Acting Professor of Greek. In June of the following year, at Mann's suggestion, the trustees offered Craig an honorary degree of Doctor of Divinity, but Craig, much surprised, declined the honor; he honestly thought himself unworthy of it. In June, 1857, Mann again urged the trustees to award this honor to Craig, and it was done. He never wished, however, to be addressed by his honorary title.

Craig spent the year 1856-57 in his parish at Blooming Grove. Early in September, 1857, Mann visited Craig and again persuaded him to come to Antioch. This time he filled the chair of Logic and Rhetoric and served as College Pastor. In urging him to become the local pastor, Mann told him: "One of your sermons would make forty such as they have been accustomed to hear." However, his health was not good and he found the work tiring. His diary of the time records long walks in the country and in the Glen, frequently in company with a girl of the senior class, Adelaide Churchill. Occasionally he spent an evening with her in the parlor of the Ladies' Hall, considering "Logic, etc." After commencement in June, 1858, Craig returned to Blooming Grove, and the following August he and Miss Churchill were married.

At Antioch Craig advocated liberal policies and methods. He urged industrial and scientific training at a time when most contemporary educators were still under the theological spell. Harwood, his chief biographer, wrote of him: "As a college professor he was a pioneer in introducing laboratory and seminar methods for the study of psychology and sociology, and as far as known was the first to have his students inspect the penal and charitable institutions and devise ways for their improvement."

As a teacher he was friendly, clear, understanding, and inspiring. One of his students, Irene Hardy, in her autobiography described a meeting with Craig on the village street. He was tall, spare, erect, his face lighted with friendship and good will;

74

while blossoms of the honey locust floated down about him, "he conversed like an archangel." Mann considered him a religious genius and said he had never known any other man who so much in character, life, and spirit, resembled Jesus Christ. His colleague, John B. Weston, said: "Large-hearted, generous, humble, even-tempered, kind, tender, unassuming, he was the most Christ-like man I ever knew."

Craig did not again return to Antioch while Mann lived. He was greatly distressed by Mann's death and at once intensified his efforts to promote the interests of the college. In June, 1862, Mann's successor, Dr. Thomas Hill, resigned to become president of Harvard, and the trustees named Craig to take charge of Antioch. During the war the college was not very active and Craig visited the campus somewhat infrequently. On one of these visits he wrote to his wife: "I arrived here, Xenia, Ohio, safely two hours ago. Shortly after arriving a stranger accosted me, and offered me a passage up with him in a carriage which he expected shortly. The carriage did not come. So he procured a locomotive and car, and we are now going up. Stranger's name is 'General Rosecrans.'" The family of General William S. Rosecrans of the Union Army then lived in Yellow Springs.

In 1865 the Unitarians raised an endowment for Antioch of $100,000, and for a while the college was in easier circumstances. However, in June, 1866, Craig asked to be relieved of the presidency, and the trustees chose Dr. G. W. Hosmer as his successor. Craig continued as a member of the faculty until 1869, though most of the time he was not in residence. From 1864 to 1869 he was a lecturer at the Meadville Theological School, giving a series of lectures each winter.

In 1869 Craig became president of the Christian Biblical Institute and continued in that post until his death, August 27, 1881. The Institute, located in Duchess County, New York, was established to help its students "search the Scriptures for themselves, with the aids and appliances of modern scholarship, and to qualify them for the free and untrammelled interpretation of the Holy Scriptures according to the individual conscience, without bias or prejudice, and to train them to be efficient ministers of the Gospel of Christ." This institution is said to have been the first theological school which did not teach theology.

In 1879 Mrs. Craig died, and Mr. Craig the following year married Dr. Sarah J. McCarn, who had been a student at Antioch under Mann and had been the second woman physician in Rochester.

Craig was not such a bitter controversialist as Mann, for his greater charity and sense of humor enabled him to realize that controversies need not be the knock-down-and-drag-out affairs Mann always made them. Speaking of one rather noisy difference of opinion, Craig said: "Five hundred years hence the echo of these loud-spoken words will be lost in the general din of small sayings."

7

A Institution in Himself

EDWARD EVERETT HALE, TRUSTEE 1865-1899

An exotic Cantabrian air flavored the Antioch commencement
of 1873. For perhaps the first and only time in the history of the
college, the ritual of awarding the diplomas to the graduates
was solemnly intoned in medieval Latin. It is true there were no
brilliant hoods of learned doctors; there were not even the plain
caps and gowns of the bachelors, for these traditional habiliments

of the scholar did not appear at Antioch commencements until special permission to wear them was granted by the faculty to the class of 1908. The simple, unpretending community avoided ritual and the unusual. Probably the college officer who thus reverted to ancient custom did so with his tongue in his cheek, conscious that he was poking fun both at the pomp of Harvard and at the blunt plainness of his audience. In the absence of President Orton, who had just resigned to accept the presidency of Ohio State University, it fell to one of the younger trustees, Edward Everett Hale, to admit the neophytes "into the company of educated men."

In gratitude for his labors in behalf of the college, Antioch had elected Hale a trustee in 1865, when as secretary of a special committee appointed by the American Unitarian Association he had turned over to the college an endowment of $100,000, raised by the committee. For thirty-four years he continued to be an active trustee, and his concern for the welfare of the college continued as long as he lived.

His father, Nathan Hale, was a nephew of the Revolutionary martyr spy and during Edward's youth was owner and editor of Boston's leading conservative newspaper, the *Daily Advertiser*. His mother was a sister of Edward Everett, professor of Greek and later president of Harvard, editor of the *North American Review*, minister to England, United States senator, and one of America's most widely known orators. Young Hale grew up in the best New England tradition. He liked others and others liked him. Writing of his early life (*Forum*, 1886), he advised young man who would have the best start in life to choose the middle place in a large family, and also a "digestion, which, as Dr. Holmes says, does not shrink from hot gingerbread just before dinner."

In the same article he said,

I owe my education chiefly to my father, my mother, and my oldest brother. I doubt if I were twelve years old when my father gave me a scrap of French, in the *Journal des Debats*, about excavations in Assyria, and asked me to translate it for his newspaper. He intrusted all of us with delicate and difficult commissions, while we ranked as boys. He gave us his entire confidence, and never withdrew it. He made me a man by treating me as a man should be treated.

Edward's father had a strong distrust of the Lancastrian system of school instruction then in vogue, in which slightly older students led the younger in a mechanical plodding through the lessons. Edward was sent to a private school kept by a simple fellow who never nagged, drove, or punished, and there Edward gained a happy scorn and contempt for all the mechanism of schools, which he retained through life. At the tender age of eight he limped through a Latin version of "Robinson Crusoe." The next year he transferred to the Boston Latin School, which he found very congenial; he always advised that boys be sent to public rather than private schools. He once said that he could not remember when he was unable to read as well as he ever could, which admittedly was never remarkably well, though he professed to be able to "understand the simpler parts of the Bible, and such passages of the newspapers as are meant to be intelligible."

In 1835 at the age of thirteen, he entered Harvard and was graduated four years later, second in his class and a member of Phi Beta Kappa. Early in his college course he became a favorite of President Quincy and was one of the best students in mathematics under Professor Peirce. He studied under Longfellow, Sparks, Palfrey, and Felton and was drilled in English composition by Professor Edward T. Channing, who numbered among his alumni such writers as Emerson, Motley, Parkman, Dana, and Holmes.

Hale was very fond of mathematics but detested Latin and Greek; he thought this was largely due to the differing methods of Professor Peirce and Professor Felton. He was not a grind and disliked the drudgery of college life. He maintained afterward that association with "good fellows" was the one benefit derived from college attendance. Later he wrote (*Forum*, 1886):

> I do not believe that any life outside a college has been yet found that will in general do so much for a man in helping him for this business of living. I could get more information out of Chambers's Encyclopaedia, which you can buy for ten dollars, than any man will acquire as facts, by spending four years in any college. But the business of changing a boy into a man, or, if you please, changing an unlicked cub into a well-trained gentleman is, on the whole, more simply and certainly done in a good college than anywhere else. . . . One comes back to Mr. Emerson's word, "It is little matter what you learn, the question is with whom you learn."

Elsewhere he wrote, "Like all college boys at their graduation, I was sternly old-school; thought Mr. Emerson half crazy; disliked abolition; doubted as to total abstinence, and in general, followed the advice of my Cambridge teachers, who were from president down to janitor, all a hundred years behind their time." He had the conservative Whig ideas of Webster, Everett, and his father.

Hale began to contribute to the *Advertiser* at the age of fifteen, chiefly reviews and editorials. He learned shorthand and developed the art of rapid and confident composition. During his senior year at Harvard he reported the sessions of the State legislature for the *Advertiser*, and though he considered the speeches to which he had to listen "all flamdiddle," he continued to cover the legislature for several years.

He had decided to enter the ministry, but he thought nothing of formal theological training. He spoke smilingly of the "Divinity drawl," and concluding that the Harvard Divinity School could not give him what he wanted, he embarked on a course of reading and self-training, with intervals of teaching at Dixwell's School in Boston, and of travel and mountain climbing. He wrote,

> Frankly, the average clergy drive me to despair; I have to forget their existence when I want to be hopeful. It is not that they are narrow; it is, that knowing what they know and reading what they read, they have no more conception that their knowledge or thought can serve

this generation, or of the way in which they can serve it, than they have of serving the people in the planet Herschel.

As a young man he was an impressive figure, tall and gaunt; his eyes were searching and appealing; his voice rich and deep and resonant. He was clever, amusing, and interesting; he kept up with current literature and tried his hand at making daguerrotypes, collecting wild flowers, and mixing chemicals.

At twenty he began to preach here and there and spent one winter preaching in Washington. At twenty-three he was called to the pastorate of the Church of the Unity in Worcester and served that congregation for ten years. In1856, at the age of thirty-four, he went to the South Congregational Church in Boston, where he was pastor until 1901, and emeritus until his death in 1909. In 1903 he became chaplain of the United States Senate.

Hale walked with the great and with the lowly. Emerson visited the Worcester study between trains and told Hale of the Browning romance. Senator Hoar frequently came to him for advice. On the other hand, Hale often passed by meetings of the privileged to carry alms and encouragement to the poor of Boston's North End. He was a pioneer in social work; he organized Boston's charities and urged upon all the necessity of "co-operative citizenship"; he preferred charity to theology, mutual assistance to arid hair-splitting. He was a staunch friend of the uneducated, the poor, the immigrant, and the Negro.

For half a century Hale was foremost among American Unitarians. He was a popular preacher, though some thought him a shade radical. He wrote over two thousand sermons, because he sought always to present fresh material. He was one of the most voluminous writers of his day, his published titles running to more than seventy. In 1854 he wrote, lectured, and raised funds to further the work of the Emigrant Aid Society in assisting Northerners to settle in Nebraska and Kansas. He had a talent for arousing enthusiasm, for organization, and for accomplishment.

The America that was to be, after the wounds of civil war had been healed, he called the New Civilization. His liberal and practical theology urged him to further popular education and to improve the lot of all men and women. So effective were his efforts that he did succeed in raising the tone of American life. It is amazing that in the middle of the last century, now nearly a hundred years ago, Hale could have taken such deep interest in the problems we are likely to consider wholly modern—in the proper and profitable use of leisure, in the choice of vocation, in the relative relief burden which should be carried by the individual, by charitable organizations, and by the state. He speculated on what would happen if Jesus should return, especially to Boston. He even wrote a book on Spain.

About the time of his appointment to the Antioch endowment committee, he published in the *Atlantic* (November, 1864) the short story which brought him most fame as an author, "The Man Without a Country." The tale carries such an air of truth that for many years Hale was forced at frequent intervals to deny that it had any basis of fact.

In furthering the New Civilization, Hale interested himself in the work of the Soldier's Memorial Society which sought to furnish means for the industrial education of the Southern whites. Hale frequently visited these schools in Richmond and in Wilmington, N.C., and now and then inspected the Hampton Negro schools. In a letter from Richmond in September, 1866, he wrote:

> I have been here making a speech in behalf of the schools for poor white trash in Richmond and other Southern cities. It seems as if the Lord has opened a way for us to upset the F.F.V., and so I hope all the gentry of the South, by the elevation of the mud sills. . . . I wish I could hold my beloved A.U.A. up to this work of disentangling the Southern web, but they are still ecclesiastical and believe in tracts and black morocco sermon-cases. *Tasit pio.* But for a' that we will make them do all we can, and make Antioch do much more, get in our free schools in Richmond, Wilmington, and Charleston, and be ready for a new Antioch in Florida and Georgia.

Early in 1865 Hale wrote to his brother Charles that the Unitarians hoped "to re-establish Antioch College, under our own men, and to lure into the ministry by this means and by the attraction of its greater activities, men enough to run our enlarged machinery," and to extend a liberal theology and to educate men who would push the work of the liberal church.

Prior to receiving the $100,000 endowment from the Unitarians, Antioch had practically no resources. When the money was made available in the summer of 1865, the buildings were repaired, and a special committee looked about for a suitable president and faculty. The presidency was offered to General James A. Garfield, who declined; to Andrew D. White, who felt a commitment to Cornell and who also declined; to John A. Andrew, governor of Massachusetts and president of the American Unitarian Association, who after some hesitancy also declined. Acting-President Craig was prevailed upon to carry on for another year, and in 1866 Dr. George W. Hosmer became president.

In July, 1866, Hale wrote, "I did not get to Antioch, and the Trustees in a savage fit of economy razed the staff pretty badly." Most of the faculty were released, among them William F. Allen, for many years after a distinguished teacher at the University of Wisconsin; Francis Tiffany, minister and author; John W. Langley, afterward an accomplished chemist and metallurgist at the University of Michigan; and Theodor Suliot, later president of Avery Institute.

But after two years had passed Hale was more optimistic; he wrote to his brother Charles,

> We are well pleased with our year's success at Antioch. The spirit and character of the men employed and the women, have been such as to lift the school wholly above the level of a mere sectarian academy, and we are now quite independent of the intrigues of the Christian sect or any others. We have in the last year increased our endowment near $10,000; we have increased the income from scholars, the real test of success, $1700; and with this real prosperity have been able to collect, almost without solicitation, about five thousand dollars for running expenses of the institution. I call it *school* because I think that is beginning to be the respectable name. In truth the age of the scholars averages more than that of those at Cambridge. The professors are young and have their reputations to make,

eager to see the institution succeed so that they do twice as much work as the men at Cambridge seem to me to do. Off there by themselves, there is indeed no temptation to them to do otherwise.

The Unitarians, probably at the suggestion of Hale, supplied a small sum yearly to provide for a series of lectures at Wilberforce University. Many of these lectures were given by members of the Antioch faculty.

In 1874 the presidency was offered to Rev. J. F. Moors but he declined. Hale wrote to Mrs. Hale in December,

I am at the last disappointed by this letter. They had a rumor about Yellow Springs that he was coming. There is this about it, however, if he cannot see that the opportunity is something much larger than the presiding over a boarding school of a hundred and fifty scholars, if he cannot see that it involves, in the best hands, the moral and physical direction of the public education of the state of Ohio, and for that matter of the neighboring states, probably he would not make it do that. When we blame the man who makes through cowardice the great refusal we forget that only the man who is born to set the world right can set it right; and that for an apprentice, quite incompetent, to put his tool into the running of the watch, will most likely smash the whole.

The great hopes which Hale had for Antioch were to be realized only in a small degree during his life. He came to the campus nearly every year during the third of a century he was a member of the Board of Trustees; he came to hearten the faculty and the students and to keep the college directed on the liberal path. Frequently he read from his own work before meetings of the literary societies, most often from "My Double, and How He Undid Me." Benevolent, enthusiastic, energetic, he found a use for his powers in the many enterprises which claimed his attention. He was, as Moncure Conway justly observes in his *Autobiography*, "an institution in himself."

8

The Apprenticeship of G. Stanley Hall

1872-1876

In June, 1872, James Kendall Hosmer resigned as Professor of Rhetoric and English Literature at Antioch to take a similar position at the University of Missouri. For a few weeks following his resignation he was in New York City and there renewed his friendship with G. Stanley Hall, whom he had met in Berlin in 1869. At Professor Hosmer's suggestion, President George

W. Hosmer, his father, appointed Hall to the vacant professorship.

At the age of twenty-six, G. Stanley Hall joined the Antioch faculty as professor of Rhetoric and English Literature. The following year he was made Bellows Professor of Mental Philosophy and English Literature and held that chair for the next three years.

These were truly apprentice years for the alert, versatile, and handsome young instructor, who had not yet determined upon a career. Confessing later that his life had been "a series of fads and crazes,"[1] he recognized that at Antioch he had discovered two of the major phases of his subsequent work—the application of evolutionary concepts to mind growth, and the subjection of psychology to laboratory investigation.[2]

Granville Stanley Hall was born in Ashfield, Franklin County, Massachusetts, February 1, 1846. His parents were farmers, descendants of the Brewsters and Aldens of Plymouth. In rearing their three children, the Halls sought to bring out the latent abilities and interests of each by means of such family enterprises as a group newspaper, an orchestra, a discussion circle, and a sort of lyceum system of reading aloud. Although it was recognized that Stanley had little musical ability, he was given lessons in piano, organ, and violin. His mother wished him to become a minister and therefore provided training in music and public speaking.

Prepared in Williston Seminary in Easthampton, Stanley entered Williams College in 1863, walking the greater part of the distance from Ashfield to Williamstown. He seems to have played no outstanding part among the two hundred students there. Although he ranked below the middle of his class in 1865, his work improved and he was elected to Phi Beta Kappa in his senior year. Of the twelve members of the faculty, he was influenced most by Professor Bascomb, who, although he held the chair of rhetoric, was far more interested in philosophy and political economy. Hall was unable to win a place on the college baseball team but was granted membership in societies devoted to music, natural history, theology, art, chess, journalism, and elocution. Near the end of his sophomore year he was somewhat reluctantly "converted" and joined the college church; he did not "turn Unitarian" for fear of wounding his mother. The president of Williams, Mark Hopkins, thought Hall's religious views too heterodox. During this period he has been described as a youth of gentle gravity, a good conversationalist, with warm regard for friends but a morbid bashfulness of girls—an attitude that changed little in later years. "Always a little afraid of women, he manifested in their presence a courtliness and charm of manner which delighted them utterly."[1]

The young Williams graduate spent the winter of 1867-68 at Union Theological Seminary. During these months in New York he saw many plays and operas. He heard all the great preachers of the day. His own trial sermon at the Seminary was so heterodox that the venerable president, Dr. Skinner, instead of giving the usual gentle criticism, felt moved to offer a prayer in his behalf. Henry Ward Beecher thought his young friend more interested in philosophy than in theology, and through the generosity of a parisioner, provided funds for a period of study in Germany.

Hall entered Bonn in the autumn of 1868 and at Christmas transferred to Berlin, where he filled five semesters with wildly chosen electives, including philosophy, physiology, anthropology, theology, and Greek. He was influenced by the prevailing Darwinian philosophy and became engrossed in the works of Huxley and Goethe.

In 1871 he returned to America, certain of appointment to the chair of logic and ethics at Minnesota, but the president unexpectedly cancelled the agreement, declaring that Hall was too "Germanized" and likely to "unsettle men and teach them to hold no opinions." Hall then returned to the Seminary, from which he was graduated B.D. in 1871, and became a private tutor, studying the history of philosophy in leisure time.

During the first year of his professorship at Antioch, he lived in the President's House with the family of Dr. Hosmer, who retired as president on January 1, 1873, but remained until June as Channing Professor of History and Ethics. After the Hosmers moved away from the village, Hall roomed in the home of Col. Joseph Wilson, in a large brick house on East Limestone Street.

Hall found the natural surroundings of the college delightful and formed the habit of walking in the Glen and along the country roads. He wrote:[3]

> The scenery in the vicinity was beautiful, as the college was situated near the edge of a very deep and long ravine and near a famous chalybeate spring, beside which an immense summer hotel had been built. The beautiful walks were always tempting to the students, and the chief disciplinary cases which came before the conservative faculty were the results of incessant "pairing off" of the boys and girls for afternoon and evening rambles.

He took delight in the high ideals of the college community and in the keenness of the intellectual atmosphere. No sharp line was drawn between the more mature students and the faculty. The instructors were young, alert, and progressive. Among them were Samuel C. Derby (Latin), later president of Antioch and dean at Ohio State; John B. Weston, '57 (Greek), later president of the Christian Biblical Institute; Rebecca S. Rice, '60 (mathematics and astronomy); Edward Orton (natural science), later first president of Ohio State; Edward Claypole (natural science), later a professor at Buchtel and at Throop Institute of Technology; and Charles Chandler (chemistry and physics), for many years at Ripon College. President Hosmer was succeeded by Professor Orton, who resigned in June, 1873, to take up his duties at Ohio State. After the presidency had been declined by John Farwell Moors, a prominent Unitarian minister of Somerville, Professor Derby became acting president. Hall observed:[3] "Although it was small, the little faculty was very ambitious to do the best work possible and there was much talk about 'maintaining Harvard standards.' "

As a graduate of a men's college, Hall was alert in his observations of coeducation. He says:[3]

> We had a select body of mature young ladies who came from a wider area and were, on the whole, superior to the men, who were more local. . . . I was always impressed with the way in which the strong feminine element dominated the college sentiment, and felt that the active boy student life that characterized other non-coeducational institutions was lamentably lacking because of this.

Concerning his Antioch days, Hall wrote:[5]

> My chair was a whole settee. I taught English language and literature, German, French, philosophy in all its branches, preached, was impressario for the college theater, chorister, and conducted the rhetorical exercises, and spread out generally. But I did a lot of solid reading in spite of all these duties, and my four years at Antioch were most profitable ones.

Included in the course in English Literature was a section on Anglo-Saxon, and for this Hall was forced to do considerable cramming. After the retirement of President Hosmer, Hall took all classes in philosophy, and for the remaining three years at Antioch philosophy was his chief interest. He says:[3] "I was able to devote most of my time to teaching philosophical subjects as I would. I was an enthusiast for Darwin, Spencer, and Huxley, and as the religious spirit was free I could do practically what I would."

It had been the custom from the founding of the college for the faculty to take turns in conducting chapel, but during Hall's professorship there seems to have been a different arrangement. On June 24, 1874, the trustees formally thanked Professors Hall and Weston for their charge of the college pulpit and requested them "to continue this service till a preacher is appointed, and that in slight recognition of their service the Treasurer be required to pay to each of them $100." Frequently in the absence of the organist, Hall was called upon to play the organ also. As director of the college choir,[5] he required punctual attendance in the classroom, and through his knowledge of the best music, and untiring efforts, he brought the choir to a rank never since attained. Some members ventured to protest against the frequent use of *Ein' Feste Berg* for chapel exercises, saying, "We do not like it." "Then sing it until you do," was Professor Hall's firm reply.

It was the rule at Antioch that the Professor of English Literature act also as librarian. Hall did considerable work in caring for the small collection of books and was especially interested in arranging the papers and pamphlets relating to the history of the college. It would be interesting to read today the speech he gave before the Crescent Literary Society in 1876 on "The Past, Present, and Future of Antioch College."

He became interested in the student dramatic organization and was placed in charge of the four Shakespearean productions given yearly. He states[3] that the plays were presented in the chapel (Antioch Hall Auditorium), "the platform of which was expressly built that it might be used as a stage for the benefit of the literary society. I had to choose and cut the play, assign the parts, prepare the scenery, suggest the costumes to the young women who made them, and act in every way as impressario."

Professor Hall also held "rhetorical exercises" in the evenings; he listened to and criticized the work of students interested in public speaking—and in those days everyone was eager to acquire facility in "oral English." There were three literary societies, two composed of men (the Star and the Adelphian Union) and one of women (the Crescent). These societies gave weekly programs consisting of readings, original essays and poems, debates, and a "newspaper." The grade of work done under Hall's direction was outstanding. A signal honor came to Antioch in the spring of 1876 when the second prize in the Interstate Oratorical Contest, held in Chicago, was awarded to Laura Ann Kent (Mrs. H. S. Foster) for her oration, "Beatrice and Margaret." This Antioch student was the only woman contender; she competed with the future senators Albert J. Beveridge of Indiana and Robert M. La Follette of Wisconsin —and won.

Hall also had charge of the essays prepared by the graduates each year for the commencement exercises. He voluntarily assumed the same task for the students at Wilberforce, with gratifying results. At that time the American Unitarian Association yearly granted $400 for a series of lectures at Wilberforce by Antioch instructors. Among these, Hall talked in a popular vein about the great figures of literature and art. Bishop Payne was then president of Wilberforce, and cordial relations existed between the two institutions.

> He took ready part in teacher's institutes and conventions with other members of the faculty, and was instrumental in having them held at the college. Being a free and easy speaker, with new ideas, he was listened to with interest and pleasure and lectured in the neighboring cities on such occasions.
>
> He not only entered into college activities with enthusiasm, but also into the social life of the village, organizing at one time a literary club of college and towns-people, with a regular public program of real worth and attractiveness. There was much narrow sectarian prejudice and some bitter opposition, both within and outside the college, to Professor Hall's theological views. . . . He was kind, impulsive, energetic, very sensitive and often misunderstood.[5]

When it appeared that the "Great American Literary Bureau," an undercover organization supplying themes and other papers to college students throughout the country at a stiff fee, was located in Yellow Springs, Hall volunteered to undertake an investigation on behalf of the faculty. His anticipation of the danger involved was fully realized:[3]

> When I happened to meet the leader of the organization on the street he took a revolver from his pocket and loaded it while passing me. Later, a bullet fired in my direction lodged in the post of the store a safe rod from where I was; another was fired through the window of my room a few nights later; while at a rhetorical evening exercise where I was on the platform, a bottle of acid was thrown through the window, evidently directed at me but fell short and broke

on the edge of the platform, spoiling my clothes and the dresses of some of the girls in the front row.

Concerning friends made at Antioch he says:[3]

> I greatly enjoyed the friendship here of my colleague, Professor Rebecca S. Rice, head of the mathematics department, who had studied in Germany and was a lady of great ability and refinement. Although she was much older than I [ten years], we struck up a great intimacy, not only in college but in town and church matters. I treasure highly the memory of this acquaintance, which lasted not only during my stay here but for many years after she had established a successful private school for girls in Chicago. Here, too, I formed the slight acquaintance of Cornelia Fisher, who was later to be my wife, whose father had retired from business in Cincinnati and lived in town upon a modest income. . . . At commencement not only the local but our most distinguished Eastern trustees, Dr. Edward Everett Hale and Dr. Bellows of New York, and Robert Collier, another trustee, were generally present for a few days and gave several addresses. They were all very companionable with the instructors.

Hall's first venture in the short-story, "A Leap-Year Romance,"[4] was written during his last year at Antioch. He submitted it to *Appleton's Journal*, and received $150 upon its acceptance, though the story did not appear until late in 1878. There is no doubt that he had in mind the campus and the personnel at Antioch. Upon the publication of the story he was sharply criticized, somewhat to his own astonishment, for the thinness with which he had disguised the locale and the characters. For example:

> Springtown City is a quiet little village that has grown up around a college for both sexes, which was founded by a vigorous religious sect, something less than half a century ago, in what was then the far West. It stands upon a gentle southern slope, from which, across a deep ravine or glen, can be seen a magnificent expanse of rich level bottom-land.

The story is centered upon the love between Professor Moors, a studious, diligent pedagogue who is firmly committed to the doctrine of the superiority of the male and the domestic subjection of women, and Josephine Newell, a graduate of the college, aged twenty-eight, as firmly committed to the cause of equal rights. We see them at meetings of the Springtown Literary Club, on walks in the Glen and on country roads, at the New Year reception in the college parlors, at afternoon teas, at a lecture by "Dr. Skinner." One of their walks takes them "along the icy glenroad, following the glen around a curve of several miles, and home by an unfrequented road over the hill past the spring and the old hotel." His attitude brings about a coolness between them. At last Miss Newell sends a note suggesting a compromise in points of view, but the flinty professor seems to require capitulation. Rebuffed, she goes to Ashton and there founds an institute for young ladies. A year later she writes to ask him to speak before her pupils, and he agrees on the condition that she in turn will speak before the teacher's institute at the college. Familiar scenes greet her in Springtown; "there were the tinclad spires and brick minarets of the main college-building, and the red walls of the dormitories half-covered with American ivy, dyed with all the hues of autumn." As in good melodrama, trouble follows trouble, until a nervous collapse sends Miss Newell to Europe; after failing to find solace in art, she decides to take the veil. The happy ending comes with the arrival of the frantic professor and his abject pleas that all be forgiven.

In 1874 appeared Wundt's *Grundzüge der Physiologischen Psychologie*, and this book Professor Hall read and re-read. He decided to resign and go to Leipzig to study in Wundt's laboratory. The trustees urged him to remain another year, pleading their inability to fill his place. In June, 1876, he left Yellow Springs with savings from his $1500 salary, bound for Europe. In Cambridge, however, President Eliot offered him a tutorship in English. He remained there two years, although he found his work at Harvard very monotonous after Antioch. He did graduate work in psychology under James and in physiology under Bowditch, and with the acceptance of his thesis, "The Muscular

Perception of Space," became in 1878 the first to receive the Ph.D. degree at Harvard. He then went abroad, studying for a year at Berlin under Helmholtz and Kronecker, and then at Leipzig under Wundt and Ludwig; later he went to Vienna and to Paris, where he worked under DuBois Reymond.

He returned to America, and after a year of lecturing at Harvard, Williams, and Johns Hopkins, was appointed Professor of Pedagogy and Psychology at Johns Hopkins in 1882, the first professor of pedagogics in America. The same year he set up in Baltimore the first laboratory in experimental psychology in the United States. In 1887 he founded *The American Journal of Psychology*, the first of its kind in English.

From 1888 to 1920 he served as first president of Clark University. His strong insistence made Clark coeducational. Under his leadership the students there did outstanding work in the graduate field.[7] Among Hall's students at Johns Hopkins were Dewey, Cattell, Jastrow, Sanford, Patrick, and Hyslop; and at Clark, Terman, Starbuck, and Blanchard.

Dr. Hall was described as the perennial adolescent, filled with hope and faith, zest and courage, curiosity and spontaneity. Both a mystic and a scientist, he was never wholly either. He looked upon death as a complete blotting out; he fought off death because he loved life and because there were so many books yet to be written. At last when he realized that he was a dying man,[1]

> he managed to light his last cigar with the air of one who had never had so good a smoke before, and went to his accepted annihilation grandly, with courtesy that did not fail, with nonsense on his lips and courage in his heart.

He died in Worcester April 24, 1924.

In a letter to President Arthur E. Morgan, December 23, 1921, Dr. Hall said:

> I spent four very pleasant and profitable years there, and have never been back except for one hasty call. . . . You are certainly doing wonderful things for Antioch. Even in my day it stressed quality and standards above numbers, and I am greatly pleased to know that

it can do so yet, and so justly. . . . It was there that I had my first craze for evolution generally and took a turn towards experimental or laboratory psychology. . . . It was all poor cheap work, and I certainly matured during those four years as I never did anywhere else, even in my six years abroad, so that I count myself a loyal son of Antioch.

BIBLIOGRAPHY

[1] Pruett, Loraine. *G. Stanley Hall, a Biography of a Mind.* N.Y., Appleton, 1926.
[2] Letter to President Morgan, Dec. 23, 1921.
[3] Hall, G. S. *Life and Confessions of a Psychologist.* N.Y., Appleton, 1924.
[4] Hall, G. S. "A Leap-Year Romance." *Appleton's Journal,* 1878.
[5] Wilson, L. N. *G. Stanley Hall, a Sketch.* N.Y., Stechert, 1914.
[6] Hall, G. S. *Recreations of a Psychologist.* N.Y., Appleton, 1920.
[7] Hamilton, A. E. "Stanley Hall, a Memory." *American Mercury,* II, 7, pp. 287-292, July 1924.

Antiochiana in
The Olive Kettering Library

By LOUIS FILLER

When Arthur E. Morgan, in 1920, took Antioch College in hand and set out to revitalize it, he had little time to spare for its history. Antioch College still retained a tradition composed of famous names and accomplishments, as the preceeding essays show, and first of all of Horace Mann. But the College was threadbare in all material respects and urgently in need of a program. The latter Mr. Morgan was prompt to provide, and behind it he put a force of character and energy which peopled the campus with resourceful faculty and students. In so vital an atmosphere, there was little time to look to the past, let alone build upon it, and it is therefore a matter which should interest future investigators concerned for Antioch's progress, why the College's career in the 1920's should seem so similar in spirit and even details to its career in the 1850's: earnest, experimental, highly moral, yet also determined upon practical results. Students of the College's history are bound to compare the personalities and minds of the two founders, Mann and Morgan, but they will also be wise to ponder local factors and conditions, especially of southwestern Ohio, for their direct or indirect effects upon the College.

They will, certainly, wish to peruse the College records in preparing their estimates, and will be grateful to Miss Bessie L. Totten, of the Class of 1900, who made their preservation her care and concern. While the College wrought, she remembered; and Antiochiana, a section of the Olive Kettering Library, which she served as Curator, is largely her creation. The holdings of Antiochiana, except for two major collections which will be separately discussed, are presently less than they may become; but even in their present state, they merit attention.

Among those holdings can be found some of the original records of the College: its day books; its class records—Antiochians, proud of their institution's pioneer work in coeducation, like to point to Jane Andrew's name in the college register of 1853: she was the first student to register; records of the student societies: the Crescent, the Union, the Star; the trustee's records and minutes; and other such materials. Here, too, can be found material, original and otherwise, bearing on the College presidents and other notables, outstandingly, of course, Horace Mann. Incidentally, these materials were implemented by Mr. Morgan himself during the 1920's, when a lucky discovery of Mann manuscripts and autographed books in Washington, D.C., brought them to the campus. Here, too, may be found alumni files; scrapbooks of news clippings about Antioch; the records of Community Government, one of the College's more famous creations; and some unique materials which may ultimately be made into publications of one sort or another. Thus, Antiochiana possesses a collection of letters and manuscripts by Irene Hardy, an early graduate of the College, and later a teacher at Stanford University; these include an autobiographical manuscript, "The Making of a School Mistress." They also include the "memory books" of another graduate, Addie (Shepard) Badger whose story Straker has told (see page 43). There is also an original manuscript by Stephen F. Weston, an Antioch dean and professor, a "History of Antioch College," which will in time repay scrutiny.

Materials from what has been called the Old College Library, to distinguish them from later accessions, are also part of Antiochiana. The collection grows as it is augmented by the productions of contemporary Antioch professors. It contains works directly relevant to Antioch's career, such as Ira W. Allen's polemical *Histor of the Rise, Difficulties and Suspension of Antioch College*

(1858), and such strictly local history as that by William Albert Galloway, of the Class of 1894, *The History of Glen Helen* (1932), so significant in College history. Numerous other books bear upon College history and interests. It is appropriate that an early institutional innovator in coeducation should have a collection of books dealing with notable women and their causes. There is, in Antiochiana, also the core of a collection of Ohio materials. These and other collections, for example of materials in the history of education and in the history of the Christian and Unitarian Churches, so significant in College affairs, will doubtless be supplemented as Antiochiana attracts an increased number of researchers who wish to explore these themes. Antiochiana could utilize additional publications bearing on the College itself, and also upon its environs: Greene County, nearby Springfield, and some materials bearing generally on southwest Ohio. Thus, it would be helpful to have readily available files of the *Xenia Torchlight* and other local publications which, early in the nineteenth century, and through changes of name, lit up not only the news of the area, but of the nation as well, thanks to the industrious shears of the editors who perused the exchange newspapers which came to their offices from everywhere.

The Arthur E. Morgan Papers

Recently Antiochiana acquired a major group of papers and publications: those of Mr. Morgan, who has continued to make Yellow Springs his headquarters, since he resigned the College presidency, and to participate in the College's program. Mr. Morgan earlier gave the College some of his materials—those, for example, which had gone into his preparation of a biography of the writer and social dreamer, Edward Bellamy—and, of course, some of Mr. Morgan's own papers as president of the College are part of its records. He has now turned over to it the papers in his possession which cover many of the most significant aspects of his career as engineer, educational innovator and administrator, theoretician of the "small community," and first chairman and architect of the Tennessee Valley Authority. These papers are at present in process of cataloguing. It can be expected that when they have been opened for public examination, they will influence students in the several fields indicated, and in others.

Several of the areas which the papers cover might be noticed more particularly. They include the files, except those still active, of Community Service, Inc., an organization founded by Mr. Morgan to offer advice and information to small towns and individuals interested in opening small businesses. Mr. Morgan believes that such operations can serve not only as a brake on monopoly, but can be profitable in their own right. Indeed, the town of Yellow Springs is itself outstanding in the amount of small business it can claim. It even includes a small monopoly! —not connected with the College, the Antioch Bookplate Company. The College now possesses, in Mr. Morgan's gift, an additional invaluable hoard of materials relevant to its own history, and also to Mr. Morgan's important educational contributions elsewhere. For example, a consultant (1948-1949) to the University Education Commission of the Government of India, Mr. Morgan helped set up no fewer than thirteen universities with individualized programs intended to modify the country's present, traditional curriculum.

Mr. Morgan's activities, which the files reflect, feature influential trips to Finland, Africa, Mexico, and numerous locales in the United States. It is not easy, or necessary, to distinguish his work as an engineer from that as a "social engineer." His labors as builder of the Miami Conservancy District, following the disastrous flood of 1913 in Dayton, Ohio, was a first draft of his later plans for the T.V.A. His work on a water control project in New Mexico, in 1925, involved him in the politics necessary to securing passage of a conservancy bill. All in all, Mr. Morgan has helped administer from fifty to seventy-five water control projects. One of the most recent and most newsworthy has linked conservation to the problem of justice for the Seneca Indians. The collection is enriched by the manuscripts of all of Mr. Morgan's writings (an introductory selection from them is planned by the College), as well as biographical materials, and others bearing on Mr. Morgan's personal relations.

THE STRAKER COLLECTION

This leaves for notice what is in many ways the foundation stone of Antiochiana, since, thanks to the efforts of Robert L. Straker, it does so much to bind together the significant Antioch themes, in terms of original materials, and also in terms of analysis, historical perspective, and that concern for the large and small factors which must go into the building of a significant institution. Mr. Straker was no specialist. He could absorb himself in the details of Horace Mann's life, or in those of Horace Mann's son, or again, in the negotiations which accompanied fund-raising for the new college in Ohio which invited Mann to be its first president. Antioch in the post-Mann era held Straker's attention as fully as did the more glamorous years of the 1850's. His interest in Antioch extended through his own years as a student in Yellow Springs, and beyond into the present era. He kept up with the College's changes in program and personnel as an historian as well as an affectionate and highly regarded alumnus.

His papers reflect the catholicity of his interests, and also of his regard for Antiochiana. He early took to making gifts, especially of his own researches into Mann; but, in addition, he kept in regular touch with Miss Totten, and with others of the Antioch staff of teachers and administrators who might be involved in details of Antioch history and Antioch contacts with the outside world; these sometimes became considerable, as during the Centennial year of 1953.

Straker industriously copied Mann, Peabody, and other materials in major repositories, and also developed a bibliographer's knowledge of sources and materials. Steadily, and out of what was after all a relatively modest income, he purchased books, manuscripts, and ephemera to create a library of materials for which researchers will be increasingly grateful.

The heart of his collection is the chronicle of direct data and related information which he began to build, first in furtherance of his projected life of Horace Mann, then of his projected study of the Peabody Sisters, and especially the most individual and significant of the three: Elizabeth P. Peabody, and, finally, of his projected history of Antioch College. His nine typescript volumes of Mann materials included an index invaluable to the student of the subject, and reflected their author's high clarity of purpose and organization. Straker's materials continued to grow, and to deepen; he was reluctant to put a time-limit on his studies, fascinated by byways of genealogy, town histories, local and national events relevant to the lives of his subjects. He published relatively little. His organization of materials next took in Elizabeth P. Peabody, and notes for a history of Antioch College. At his death, the Mann volumes had become thirty-four, with a new index and a new supplement to the new index. The Elizabeth P. Peabody binders finally ran to fourteen volumes, plus a volume of index; Straker had earlier given Antiochiana a seven-volume set. Finally, there were "Notes for a History of Antioch," in three volumes, part of the third being an index. Furthermore, hand-written notes interspersed through the volumes indicate that he had by no means abandoned his interest in gathering additional materials and inserting them in his collections.

It merits emphasis that this was a creative achievement; the chronicles have form and substance. Ultimately, an editor can abstract from them several useful volumes for publication which will give a sense of Straker's industry and imaginative grasp of his subjects. Indeed, interwoven with the materials are creative historical essays which can be culled almost directly for publication; this is the case with the unpublished article, "Benevolence in the Heroic Degree" (1935). There is also, among other materials, a more elaborate and documented version of Straker's published essay, *The Unseen Harvest,* which could serve scholars. Particular mention should be made of rough drafts of three chapters which Straker prepared for his biography of Mann, dealing with "Slavery and Congress," "Mann's First Speech in Congress," and "The Drayton and Sayres Trial," the latter an account of one of the most famous of fugitive-slave affairs.

Straker left a number of manuscripts which can be considered as publishing ventures in due course. These include:

"Letters of Mann and Charlotte Messer Mann, 1829-1832," a delightful compilation, reflecting the courtship and relationship which Mann and his first wife experienced until her tragic death.

"Gloss upon Glosses," a detailed, page-by-page commentary and criticism of Louise Hall Tharp's *The Peabody Sisters of Salem* (1950), and *Until Victory: Horace Mann and Mary Peabody* (1953): an informative and even amusing review of details separated by dots, somewhat reminiscent of Thomas Beer's *The Mauve Decade,* in its exploitation of curiosa.

"Horace Mann, 1844-1868," a curious monograph dealing with the interest of Mann's son in botany; it includes an essay by Straker on Thoreau, and was prepared for the Department of Botany, Cornell University, 1956.

"Directory of Faculty and Other Officers of Antioch College, 1850-1936."

Straker collected books, magazines, and other current materials, and combed bookdealers catalogs for materials from the past. The one hundred and eighty volumes of books Antiochiana has acquired were intended for his work, and vary from readily obtained items to such less available productions as Robert L. Black's *The Little Miami Railroad* (n.d.); [Anna Cabot Lowell] *Theory of Teaching, with a Few Practical Illustrations, By a Teacher* (1841); William B. Fowle's *The Teacher's Institute* (1847); John B. O'Neal's *The Annals of Newberry* (1859); *The Record of Births, Marriages and Deaths, . . . in the Town of*

Dedham [Mass.] ... *1635-1845* (1886); and a variety of relevant pamphlets: all in all, a desirable addition to Antiochiana materials.

However, the compiler also worked so steadily and energetically to photograph Mann, Peabody, and other materials, that such subjects can be pursued with profit in the library; and, in addition, Straker himself acquired original materials, notably correspondence, which students in his subject area will wish to consult.

This brief description of Antiochiana and of the Straker Collection should not conclude without noting the folders of Strakeriana—letters, notes, negotiations respecting book and other purchases, information, and historical discussion—which reveal his pleasant and scholarly nature, his useful and interesting pursuits.